FIGHTING IRISH

THE MIGHT, THE MAGIC, THE MYSTIQUE OF NOTRE DAME FOOTBALL

BY
RON SMITH
JOE HOPPEL

SportingNews
BOOKS

PHOTO CREDITS

T = Top B = Bottom L = Left R = Right C = Center

CONTRIBUTING PHOTOGRAPHERS

The Sporting News Archives: Cover (background), 4-5, 6-7, 12-13, 15, 16-17, 18, 19, 36-37, 44TC, 55, 78T, 80, 83, 84, 89B, 91BC, 101, 104, 107, 158-59, 174-75, 178-79, 195L, 217BR, 221B

Albert Dickson/The Sporting News: 38, 220, Cover B

Bob Leverone/The Sporting News: 42T, 44TL, 196T

August Miller/The Sporting News: 28

Dilip Vishwanat/The Sporting News: 24, 29, 30B, 31, 42B, 93B

John Cordes for The Sporting News: 26BL, 26BR, 27, 223TC, 223BL

Ross Dettman for The Sporting News: Cover C (Willingham), 14B, 30T, 33B, 47TL 222B, 223TR, 223BR

Sam Greenwood for The Sporting News: 32, 147L

University of Notre Dame Sports Information Office: 21, 33T, 39B, 40BL, 41T, 41B, 43, 44B, 45T, 50, 51TL, 51R, 52L, 54, 56, 57, 61T, 63, 66, 69, 70L, 70R, 71T, 71B, 74, 75, 76, 79, 81, 88, 91T, 92TR, 92B, 93T, 103, 110T, 110C, 110B, 111L, 111R, 112TL, 112TR, 112BR, 113TR, 113BL, 113BR, 114TL, 114C, 114B, 115T, 115BR, 116T, 116BL, 116BR, 117T, 117B, 118, 119T 119B, 120TL, 120TR, 120B, 121T, 121B, 122TL, 122-23B, 123T, 124T, 124C, 124B, 125TL, 125C, 125B, 126T, 126C, 126L, 126-27B, 127TL, 127TR, 127BL, 128L, 128R, 128B, 129TL, 129TR, 129BR, 130TL, 130TR, 130C, 131TR, 132TL, 133TL, 133TR, 133BL, 134TL, 134TR, 134B, 135L, 135BL, 136L, 136BR, 137BL, 137BR, 138TL, 138L, 139BR, 140BR, 141TR, 143BL, 143BR, 144T, 144B, 145TL, 146TL, 146R, 146BL, 146BR, 147B, 154-55, 164B, 168, 169, 169TL, 169TC, 169TR, 169BL, 175B, 175L, 175TR, 180, 184-85, 188-89, 189B, 194TL, 194TR, 195T, 195TR, 195R, 195B, 200B, 200 BL, 201L, 201BR, 202L, 202R, 202BR, 202-03T, 204L, 204R, 205BR, 206TL, 206R, 207L, 207BR, 208B, 210B, 211C, 211BL, 211BR, 212C, 213T, 214TL, 214R, 215TR, 215R, 215BL, 216B, 217L, 218L, 218C, 218R, 218B, 219TL, 220L, 220R, 221T, 221BL, 222T

AP/Wide World Photos: Cover L, (Knute Rockne), 8, 20, 25, 39T, 53, 59, 60-61, 68, 77T, 77B, 82, 91BL, 91BR, 92TL, 96, 97, 98, 99, 100, 102, 105, 106, 108, 112BL, 115BL, 117C, 121C, 122L, 123C, 123BR, 125TR, 142B, 145BL, 147TL, 150-51, 156-57, 157BR, 159BR, 160-61, 164-65, 172-73, 175BR, 176-77, 180-81, 186-87, 194B, 208, 209T, 209B, 210T, 212TR, 212BL, 213R, 213B, 217T, 219TR, 219C, 220T

Malcolm W. Emmons: 9, 58, 62, 65, 85, 86, 87, 109, 128T, 129BL, 130BL, 131, 132TR, 132BL, 132BR, 133BL, 135TL, 135BR, 136TR, 138R, 139TL, 139L, 139BL, 140BL, 141R, 152-53, 190, 214B, 216L, 219BL, 219BR

Joe Raymond: Cover R (Joe Montana), 14T, 47TR, 64L, 64R, 89T, 90, 137TR, 140T 141TL, 142T, 143TL, 143C, 144R, 145C, 162-63, 166B, 166-67, 182, 182-83, 190-91 194L, 196C, 205C, 205BL, 207T, 214C, 215C, 216TR

Brian Spurlock: 44TR, 45B, 46, 47B, 194-95, 197

Michael & Susan Bennett: 3, 52L, 163BR, 209R, 211R

Rudy International: 40BR, 137TL

Rich Clarkson: 160T

Courtesy of the Dan Thompson family: 67, 78B

Copyright ©2003 by The Sporting News, a division of Vulcan Sports Media, Inc., 10176 Corporate Square Drive, Suite 200, St. Louis, MO 63132. All rights reserved. Printed in the U.S.A.

ISBN: 0-89204-721-6

10 9 8 7 6 5 4 3 2 1

ACKNOWLEDGEMENTS

Having married into a family with six children, a father and a grandfather who are Domers, I make no pretense that Notre Dame is not a special place for me. In fact, the Grotto and the path around the lakes are among my favorite places on earth.

Notre Dame will always be a magical place, whether the football team wins or loses. But there's no doubt football is an integral part of the Notre Dame experience. And that's why this was such a truly special project to work on.

If you're a Notre Dame fan, you'll love this visual trip through a glorious past. If you have been to a Notre Dame game or two, I hope this book helps you relive a wonderful experience. If you haven't been to a game in South Bend, I hope it provides a taste of college football in its highest form—and prompts you to check it out for yourself.

There are a few thank yous to be handed out:

■ To the Sporting News design team led by Michael Behrens and including Chris Callan, Russ Carr, Christen Sager, Pamela Speh and Bob Parajon, who oversaw the book's design and production.

■ To the production team of Steve Romer, Pamela Speh, Vern Kasal and Russ Carr.

■ To editors and writers Ron Smith and Joe Hoppel, photo editor August Miller and intern (and Domer) Jessica Daues.

■ To John Heisler and his staff at Notre Dame's Sports Information Office.

■ To Joe Theismann for his heartfelt foreword and Sandy Sedlack, who helped put Joe's perspective on Notre Dame into words.

Steve Meyerhoff
Editorial Director

FIGHTING IRISH

The Might, the Magic, the Mystique of Notre Dame Football

SportingNews
BOOKS

CONTENTS

FOREWORD
BY JOE THEISMANN

I've been asked countless times over the years what it is that makes Notre Dame football so special.

The answer is a complex, yet simple, one.

It's so special because of its unrivaled football heritage, the ghosts of Knute Rockne and Frank Leahy, the memories of the famed Four Horsemen. It's so special because of the magic of the Gipper and Rudy.

It's so special because of the Notre Dame campus icons and landmarks known not only throughout America, but throughout the world—the leprechaun and the Irish Guard, the Grotto, the Golden Dome and Touchdown Jesus.

It's so special because of the endless stream of magical moments, which are often explained away as "Luck of the Irish," and the marching band's rousing Victory March, which is played the world over.

It's so special because of its incredible success, its 11 national championships, its seven Heisman Trophy winners, its 94 consensus All-Americans.

All true. But the real reason Notre Dame football is so special can be summed up in one powerful word: Spirit.

Those who have walked the campus, as a student, athlete, parent, alumni or fan, can feel it. There is a certain spirit about Notre Dame—in part because of all of the reasons I've laid out above—that is unmistakable and unique. It's a spirit of community and compassion that goes beyond the boundaries of the campus. It's an energy that every graduating class carries with it into the world.

And that's the reason why thousands return to South Bend every year for football home games, the reason why hundreds return every summer to the university reunion week festivities. A return visit—to the Basilica, to the old dormitory, to the lakes, to meetings with old teammates and classmates—reignites and reinvigorates that spirit, the pride, the special feeling that comes with being part of the Notre Dame society.

Capturing that spirit, in words and pictures and

Joe Theismann had plenty of time to experience the Notre Dame 'Spirit' during three varsity seasons.

feeling, is what this book is all about. Whether you are a true Domer, a subway alum or just a curious fan, I hope you'll add this incredible package of memories to your bookshelf or coffee table. And maybe you'll even hear that spirit calling you back to South Bend.

Joe Theismann #7

THE MYSTIQUE

THE MYSTIQUE

Y OU CAN'T SEE IT, TOUCH IT OR SMELL IT. BUT YOU KNOW IT'S THERE, HANGING OVER SOUTH BEND, IND., LIKE AN INVISIBLE BLANKET. NOBODY ESCAPES THE NOTRE DAME MYSTIQUE. IT TAPS INTO YOUR IMAGINATION, TUGS AT YOUR EMOTION AND WAKES UP THE ECHOES OF YOUR LONG-FADED INNOCENCE.

IT HAS BEEN THAT WAY FOR THE BETTER PART OF A CENTURY NOW, A PLACE OF THE HEART NESTLED ON THE FRINGE OF BASKETBALL MADNESS AND IN THE BOSOM OF FOOTBALL LEGEND. THE KIND OF LEGEND THAT MAKES YOU LAUGH AND CRY, MARCH AND SING, REJOICE AND PAY TRIBUTE TO NOT-FORGOTTEN

The Notre Dame aura starts with the inspirational Golden Dome, a fitting perch for the symbolic statue of Our Lady.

heroes of poetic renown. Even non-believers are overwhelmed by Notre Dame's golden aura, an almost magical sense of destiny that is energized by the most passionate students, fans and alumni this side of football heaven.

When you make that first drive down Notre Dame Avenue, take that first step on paths once walked by Paul Hornung and Joe Montana or experience the infectious, obsessive enthusiasm for the Fighting Irish on a football weekend, you've entered a dimension that only a select few sports venues can match.

"If you could find a way to bottle the Notre Dame spirit, you could light up the universe," former Fighting Irish quarterback Joe Theismann once said, an other-world allusion that doesn't seem beyond the reach of the nation's most storied Roman Catholic university.

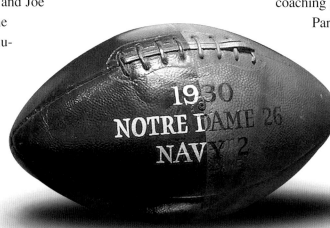

Tradition is an important thread in the Notre Dame fabric, fed by such visual reminders as a game ball from the 1930 championship season and the ever-present Leprechaun mascot.

Anybody who sets foot on the South Bend campus is quickly immersed in the legends of Knute Rockne, George Gipp, the Four Horsemen, Ara Parseghian and, of course, the most impressive string of national championship teams in college football history. Students are indoctrinated with legends of grandeur and other verbal reminders of a rich football heritage; visitors cannot escape the nationally recognized football landmarks, many of them religious statues and symbols placed strategically around the tree-lined north-central Indiana campus.

Few students complete their freshman year without intimate knowledge of

"Knute Rockne, All American," a must-view movie that captures the football passion of the former Notre Dame player and coach who guided the Irish to the first three of 11 national titles and set in motion many of the traditions that still fuel the football program today. At some point during their South Bend stay, every student also will pay homage to the coaching genius of Frank Leahy, Parseghian, Dan Devine and Lou Holtz, be inspired by the story of former Fighting Irish player Rudy Ruettiger, whose indomitable spirit was immortalized in a 1993 film, and pay poetic tribute to the Gipper and sportswriter Grantland Rice, who in 1924 penned the immortal words, "Outlined against a blue-gray October sky, the Four Horsemen rode again. ..."

Freshmen are well advised to memorize the words to the Alma Mater and Victory March because they will be asked to "wake up the echoes" thousands of times over the next four years.

Visual football images have become a more overt feature of the Notre Dame fabric. Every day, at different points on the tightly knit campus, students pass religious symbols that have become passionately associated with Fighting Irish football.

On the south wall of the 14-story Hesburgh Library, a 132-foot-high stone mosaic depicts Jesus Christ, his arms upraised, teaching a gathering of apostles, saints and scholars. The mural, visible from certain points inside nearby Notre Dame Stadium, has become known as Touchdown Jesus. Across campus stands Fair Catch Corby, a statue depicting former university president Rev. William J. Corby, his hand upraised while giving absolution to the Irish

The 132-foot stone mosaic on the south wall of the Hesburgh Library is fondly called "Touchdown Jesus."

The Grotto is a game-day stopover for players and fans who require special inspiration.

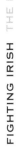

Brigade during the Civil War battle of Gettysburg. "We're No. 1 Moses" stands in flowing robes on the west side of the library, pointing skyward while chastising wayward Israelites that there is only one God.

No visit to Notre Dame is complete without a side trip to the Grotto, a stone-covered shrine to Our Lady of Lourdes on the edge of campus near St. Mary's and St. Joseph's lakes. The Grotto provides kneelers and candles to light for players and fans seeking special inspiration on game day.

Tributes to the past are everywhere, but none more conspicuous than 80,795-seat Notre Dame Stadium. Rockne helped design the single-decked oval structure before the 1930 season and it was expanded from 59,075 before the 1997 campaign. A yellow-brick facade now encloses the original red-brick outer wall,

lifesize picture-postcard campus with more than 130 architecturally distinct buildings, a faculty of more than 770 and a population (undergraduates and graduate students combined) of more than 10,000.

Father Sorin could never have conceived that his dream of providing the opportunity for a classic education, tied in theory and practice to the Catholic religion, would become so fundamentally intertwined with such a non-academic pursuit as football. But almost from the beginning—Notre Dame's one-game 1887 season against a pickup team from the University of Michigan—it was clear the sport was destined to play a special role in the school's colorful history.

Notre Dame, which named its first coach in 1894 and recorded its first eight-win season in 1901, posted a 113-31-13 record from 1887-1912, suggesting that football was already more than a sideshow diversion to the school's expanding population. But it wasn't until 1913 that Notre Dame got its first taste of national exposure, and the fact that it came on the football field instead of in the classroom became a thorny issue that

> ❝IF YOU COULD FIND A WAY TO BOTTLE THE NOTRE DAME SPIRIT, YOU COULD LIGHT UP THE UNIVERSE.❞
>
> —JOE THEISMANN

would spark much debate among present and future administrators with a more refined notion of how success should be defined.

The breakthrough came with a stunning 35-13 Notre Dame victory over powerful Army in an intersectional game at West Point, N.Y.—a win that immediately lifted the status of an upstart little school from the Midwest. College football's power base was located in the East and New York writers and fans watched in amazement as Notre Dame quarterback Gus Dorais, executing a game plan designed by new coach Jesse Harper, passed for an extraordinary 243 yards while demonstrating the potential of the still seldom-used forward pass. One of his completions was a 40-yard touchdown pass to a skinny end named Knute Rockne.

The same Rockne, of course, who would become the inspirational foundation for the college game's most revered program. "Rock" built that foundation from

which was retained as a sentimental reminder.

Football was the farthest thing from the mind of Father Edward Sorin, a 28-year-old French priest, who built his university vision in 1842 around three log cabins and the $300 he carried in his pocket. The University of Notre Dame du Lac, which once stood in isolation on the Indiana frontier, has since grown into a

1918-30 through sheer force of personality, astute football sense and a flair for the dramatic. He overwhelmed the football world with his incredible 105-12-5 record, three national championships and the idea that a little private school from Indiana could routinely embarrass the traditional powers. He charmed the nation with his wit and wholesome values. He conned fans and players with his psychological ploys. He created a legendary aura (the Four Horsemen, his Gipper speech, the "little football school that could" image) and gained immortality when he died in an icon-shattering 1931 plane crash.

While the world mourned Rockne with a John F. Kennedy-like outpouring of emotion, Notre Dame became cemented in football lore. Rock's final gift to Irish fans was a 1930 championship, achieved in the brand new stadium he had fought to build, and a legacy that refused to die when his plane went down in that Kansas wheat field. Not only did Rockne, the former chemistry teacher from Norway, create his own sports empire, he inexorably linked academics, religion and football in a mysterious trinity that sometimes defies explanation.

There's no denying Notre Dame's status as one of the country's top universities. Its overall graduation rate hovers near 94 percent, a third of its freshmen are plucked from the top five of their high school graduation classes, 75 percent of its graduates who want to attend medical school are accepted and its student body now includes students from 80 nations around the world. Notre Dame turns out doctors, judges, lawyers and legislators who make a difference in society.

But while academics builds character and prestige, football gives the school its mystical allure. It started with Rockne but has continued to build over the years despite the concerns of Notre Dame officials who have always been sensitive to

The Basilica of the Sacred Heart, with its towering steeple, blends with Notre Dame's football tradition.

the label of "football factory." De-emphasis of football was a sticky issue after Rockne's death and it remained so through the incredible 1940s and the '50s, when Leahy won an "embarrassing" 87 games and four national championships.

Even today, Notre Dame coaches are handcuffed by controls resulting from that sensitivity. They face more stringent redshirting policies than other coaches, their transfer rules are restrictive, classroom work always takes precedence over practice and football players live among the student population, not in lavish athletic halls. For 45 years, from the 1925 Rose Bowl to the 1970 Cotton Bowl, the Irish were not allowed to play in postseason games because it would interfere with the educational pursuits of the student/athletes.

"To fail academically at Notre Dame, you have to not want to be there," said running back Allen Pinkett, who earned a marketing degree from 1982-85 and remains tied to the university through his work as a radio game analyst for Westwood One Network. "All the resources are there and they take great pride in graduating folks. If you think you can slide through, you're badly mistaken. They'll kick you out. They go to great lengths to not have (athletes) stand out from the other students. If you don't pass, you don't play.

"I realize what an accomplishment (my degree) is when I look at a picture of my mom and dad. My dad saw me score hundreds of touchdowns. But I had never seen him as proud as he was that day when he saw me in my cap and gown. That meant more to him than anything I could ever have done on the football field."

The religious thread ties Notre Dame academics and athletics with a neat bow. You can't escape the physical symbols—the world-recognized Golden Dome and statue of Our Lady that tops the administration building, the Basilica of the Sacred Heart steeple, Touchdown Jesus, Fair Catch Corby, No. 1 Moses—and you are exposed daily to the more esoteric reminders. Players, many of them non-Catholics, attend Mass on the morning of all games and some make weekly pilgrimages to the Grotto during football season. Leahy routinely implored his troops to win for "Our Lady," rosary beads are worn to the nub every season by nervous game-day fingers and the Alma Mater, sung as the traditional conclusion to Notre Dame pep rallies and games, was written as a tribute to the Blessed Virgin Mary.

Before the season-opening Texas A&M game in 2000, Sister Patricia Jean Garver, a 75-year-old Holy Cross nun and unlikely football motivator, delivered a rousing speech to the Irish players at the kickoff luncheon. She reminded them that nuns all over the world have Notre Dame schedules and promised that "you will get more Hail Marys than Hershey's has candy bars." Thus inspired, Notre Dame recorded a 24-10 victory.

From that 1913 win over Army and Rockne's impressive sales job to the subsequent efforts of such legendary Notre Dame figures as Leahy, Parseghian, Moose Krause and 35-year university president Rev. Theodore Hesburgh springs the most fanatical fan base known to sports. Long before the Dallas Cowboys claimed the title of "America's

Team," years before the Cowboys even existed, Notre Dame was a coast-to-coast phenomenon.

It's not just a Catholic or Irish fascination. It's not limited to former students or transplanted alumni. Notre Dame's support cuts through ethnic and religious lines, includes the so-called "subway alumni," many of whom have never even set foot on campus, and expands yearly through its pervasive radio, television and internet exposure.

The first Notre Dame game was broadcast in 1922 by WSBT, a South Bend radio station. In 2002, almost 300 stations throughout the country carried Irish games and countless more fans listened worldwide through the Notre Dame website. NBC televises every Irish home game and Notre Dame has been a part of more than 200 national telecasts since 1952. Notre Dame game replays are syndicated nationally and highlights shows are broadcast throughout the country by network and cable affiliates with the potential to reach 25 million households.

The Irish boast an alumni network of 242 clubs, including 22 in foreign countries. But that does not include the unofficial alumni groups who gather in recreation rooms, sports bars and church halls

Former university president Rev. William J. Corby is not really signaling for a fair catch, as avid Notre Dame football fans would have you think.

Passionate fans and students have lifted the nickname 'Golden Domer' to a new plateau.

across the nation. Notre Dame's "subway alumni" numbers in the millions and their football interest borders on obsessive—a fanaticism that is on display every day of the year.

The school estimates that its website averages more than a million hits per month and the *South Bend Tribune* mails out more than 6,000 subscriptions to its *Irish Sports Report*, a 28- to 32-page weekly paper (monthly during the offseason) that has kept hungry out-of-staters informed about the daily developments of Notre Dame football since 1993. Media interest was so high when Nebraska played at Notre Dame Stadium in 2000 that the school issued a record 821 credentials.

The fanaticism, perhaps, is best illustrated by attendance figures. Since 1930, amazingly, Notre Dame has attracted capacity crowds in almost 60 percent of its road games. The largest college football crowd in

> " **MY DAD SAW ME SCORE HUNDREDS OF TOUCHDOWNS. BUT I HAD NEVER SEEN HIM AS PROUD AS HE WAS THAT DAY WHEN HE SAW ME IN MY CAP AND GOWN.** "
>
> —ALLEN PINKETT

the history of the Los Angeles Coliseum (104,953) turned out for a 1947 USC-Fighting Irish game and Notre Dame has filled such large-capacity facilities as Chicago's Soldier Field (120,000), Michigan Stadium (111,523), New York's Yankee Stadium and Polo Grounds and Philadelphia's Franklin Field.

And no college sports team has been the subject of more talk shows, highlight films, books, magazine articles, movies and videos than the Fighting Irish, who have sustained Rockne's flair for the dramatic through more than seven decades of football.

In normal football circles, that's called *impressive*.

At Notre Dame, it's called *mystique*.

Football weekend at South Bend is an almost subliminal procession of images and tradition-minded tugs at the emotions. This, after all, was the breeding ground for the Four Horsemen, Seven Mules and seven Heisman Trophy winners, all of whom have been methodically threaded into the fabric of Fighting Irish lore.

Tradition is the driving force at Notre Dame, where visitors are overwhelmed by the majesty of the Golden Dome, humbled by the proud Basilica, amused by all the combination religious/football symbolism spread around campus and caught up by the game-day fanfare. They get an uplifting sense that special things have happened here—and that something special is about to happen again.

Football weekends are choreographed around the Band of the Fighting Irish, the oldest university band in continuous existence and a performer at every Notre Dame home game since 1887. It's the centerpiece of the Friday night pep rally, the loud and raucous framework for everything that follows, as well as a pregame Saturday concert and a rousing, Pied Piper-like march to the stadium.

The Notre Dame fight song provides appropriate background music and everything comes dressed in blue, gold and, of course, green—including an over-sized leprechaun. For style and effect, there's a 10-person Irish Guard, dressed to the hilt in plaid kilt and bearskin shako, and those glistening gold player helmets, freshly painted before every game.

The atmosphere is festive and alive, activities are scripted with a movie-like flair and the luck of the Irish is more like magic, both inside the stadium and out. Notre Dame is more a state of mind than a place and the school's 11 national championships and long-term success are key ingredients of that intangible mystique.

It's fun, it's electric and it's mysterious. And on the field, three-quarters of a century later, the Fighting Irish are still winning just one for the Gipper.

Notre Dame's legendary Four Horsemen were actually talented football players with the names (left to right) Don Miller, Elmer Layden, Jim Crowley and Harry Stuhldreher.

IRISH 22, MARYLAND 0 • IRISH 24, PURDUE 17 • IRISH 25, MICHIGAN 23

SH 14, PITTSBURGH 6 • IRISH 21, AIR FORCE 14 • IRISH 34, FLORIDA S

2002 SEASON

A RETURN TO GLORY

I t was a throwback moment, a rewrite of the dramatic script penned by Ara Parseghian's Fighting Irish in a storybook 1964 season. Shockingly, amazingly, tantalizingly, a suspect Notre Dame football team was 8-0, brimming with confidence after an impressive victory at Florida State and dreaming, just like old times, of a national championship. A first-year coach, just like Parseghian almost four decades earlier, was teetering on the edge of sainthood.

Parseghian's 1964 title dream burst after nine straight wins when the Fighting Irish lost their season finale to Southern California. For Tyrone Willingham, the 8-0 dream of 2002 would disintegrate into a 10-3 finish. But the byproduct of both seasons, the magic elixir sprinkled over a stagnating program by both coaches, was hope—the promise of a more Notre Dame-like future.

"The poise (Willingham) has exemplified, that's what we alums want Notre Dame to be," said Allen Pinkett, the former Irish tailback who now serves as a game analyst on the Irish's Westwood One radio network. "It's like he was born to coach at Notre Dame."

Whether born to coach the Fighting Irish or merely destined to follow some legendary footsteps, Willingham doesn't fit snugly in the Notre Dame mold. The school's first black coach lacks the flamboyant bravado of such predecessors as Knute Rockne, Parseghian and Lou Holtz, the fast-talking, quick-quipping and charismatic giants who stoked the passions of Notre Dame fans while bringing them victories and championships.

Willingham seems almost taciturn in comparison, a no-nonsense, always-in-control leader who inspires more with attitude than words. Fans looking for social finesse come away with respect for the energy, pride and dignity of a man obviously comfortable with his status and confident in his beliefs. The man his players dubbed "The Prophet" is a commanding sideline figure, a poised, focused and all-seeing master of his universe.

"Disciplined. Serious. Aggressive. Motivated," are the adjectives fired off by former Washington State coach Mike Price, who battled Willingham's Stanford teams for seven seasons from 1995-2001. "Those are pretty good characteristics for a football team to have. Tyrone's a no-nonsense guy."

Willingham demonstrated an infectious confidence when the 48-year-old coach met with his new team for the first time in January 2002, the beginning of a much-needed Notre Dame attitude overhaul. His 45-minute presentation ended when the word "WIN" flashed on a giant screen, symbolically cleansing the memory of a 5-6 season in 2001 under coach Bob Davie.

"We're going to be playing with a chip on our shoulder," predicted senior linebacker Courtney Watson, an obvious believer in the "new Irish" as the 2002 season approached. "We're not getting the level of respect we deserve. We're not ranked. This is Notre Dame. We get the best players from around the country."

From his New Year's Day 2002 introduction (above) to his poised and focused sideline demeanor (left page), Tyrone Willingham has delivered a message of hope to Notre Dame football fans.

Senior center Jeff Faine expressed the new Willingham-inspired confidence a little more succinctly. "Our expectations are always high," he said. "We want to win a national championship."

Such sentiments were like music to the ears of frustrated Irish fans, personal vindication for Kevin White, the director of athletics who hired Willingham and introduced him as the new Notre Dame coach on New Year's Day 2002. White, who had previously hired George O'Leary to fill the position, was still reeling from the stigma of the former Georgia Tech coach's messy resignation after admitting academic and athletic inaccuracies

on his resume. White breathed easier as Willingham slowly, quietly, patiently began winning the admiration of his players and gaining the respect of the always demanding faithful.

White also provided fans with testimonials from former Willingham business associates at Stanford, where he produced a 44-36-1 record and four bowl appearances over seven years as head coach, and other friends and observers who had watched him progress from assistant coaching jobs at Central Michigan, Michigan State (his alma mater), North Carolina State, Rice, Stanford and with the National Football League's Minnesota Vikings.

While quarterback Carlyle Holiday (left) struggled to get the Notre Dame offense in sync early, corner-back Vontez Duff (right) provided big-play magic with punt-return and interception-return TDs.

When White discussed Willingham, the conversation always focused on character and pride.

"The Notre Dame family prides itself in two personal characteristics: respect and humility," White said. "Ty has taken those two ideals to another level. Just by being extremely humble. Just by being himself."

The humility is on display 24 hours a day, seven days per week. The respect manifests itself more subtly. White tells how Willingham, a devout Methodist, would take the Catholic medallion handed out to Notre Dame players at every pregame Mass, string it to his shoe before the game and wear it in honor of "Our Lady."

"To me, that's more than just subscribing to the ideals of this place," White said. "That's living it. Every time I see him with one of those medals on his shoes, I get goose bumps. When I see that, I see how he's bought into Notre Dame, big time."

A heavily pro-Fighting Irish crowd of 72,903 packed into Giants Stadium at East Rutherford, N.J., on August 31 to check out Willingham in the Kickoff Classic opener against Maryland, a team ranked No. 21 in the preseason AP poll. The new Notre Dame coach unveiled his West Coast offense that day. He showcased a hard-nosed, big-play defense and superb special teams. The Irish won, 22-0, matching the shutout total over Davie's five-year coaching tenure.

The offense, directed by junior quarterback Carlyle Holiday, controlled the

> "DISCIPLINED. SERIOUS. AGGRESSIVE. MOTIVATED. THOSE ARE PRETTY GOOD CHARACTERISTICS FOR A FOOTBALL TEAM TO HAVE. TYRONE'S A NO-NONSENSE GUY."
>
> —MIKE PRICE, FORMER WASHINGTON STATE COACH

ball more than 41 minutes and Nick Setta tied a school record by kicking five field goals. The only touchdown was scored by Vontez Duff, who returned a punt 76 yards, and three Maryland drives were stopped by Shane Walton interceptions, a memorable start to a consensus All-American season for the senior cornerback.

Willingham watched silently, unemotionally evaluating and never changing his all-knowing, unsmiling expression. His team, obviously fired up for a new coach in a season opener against a ranked opponent, played with that same control and trademark poise.

"People think (the Notre Dame tradition and excitement) doesn't affect him," said younger brother Jerome. "It has. He tells me about the pep rallies and how there's nothing like it. He's emotional; he just doesn't show it."

Willingham was equally stoic September 7 as the Fighting Irish defeated Purdue, 24-17, and handed him his first win at Notre Dame Stadium. Again it was special teams and defense that did the damage

The Fighting Irish offense came alive in Game 3 when Ryan Grant rushed for 132 yards and a pair of touchdowns in a 25-23 victory over Michigan.

with Duff returning an interception 33 yards for a touchdown, Gerome Sapp and Lionel Bolen scoring TDs on fumble returns 11 seconds apart and Setta connecting on a 19-yard field goal. Even though the offense managed only 203 total yards and failed to score for the second straight week, the Fighting Irish were 2-0—and ready, apparently, for a Game 3 character builder against No. 7-ranked Michigan.

If Fighting Irish fans wanted more proof of a 2002 revival, they got it against the Wolverines. Playing again with that contagious Willingham poise, Notre Dame pulled off a 25-23 upset. The Irish offense finally got on track, and a safety and a Setta field goal provided the difference at Notre Dame Stadium. Ryan Grant ran for 132 yards and two touchdowns and Holiday scored on a three-yard keeper—Notre Dame's first offensive TDs of the season—as the Irish beat their first Top 10 opponent in four years.

The victory was secured with 21 seconds remaining when Walton intercepted a pass and slid to the ground at the Michigan 38-yard line, only minutes after he had swatted away a potential game-tying two-point Michigan conversion pass.

"It's a big win for us and our program," Holiday said. "Now we're just set to build on this." A quirk of fate allowed the Fighting Irish to build at the expense of Willingham's former teams—Michigan State, the school for which he played and coached,

and Stanford.

The Spartans were dispatched dramatically at East Lansing when reserve quarterback Pat Dillingham threw a 60-yard touchdown pass to Arnaz Battle with 1:15 remaining for a 21-17 Irish win—Notre Dame's first against Michigan State after five consecutive losses to the Spartans and an important confidence builder. "Michigan State is a huge part of me, but I'm the coach of Notre Dame," Willingham snapped at reporters after the game.

Stanford fell meekly, 31-7, at South Bend as Willingham joined Frank Leahy, Parseghian and Jesse Harper as the only Notre Dame coaches to open their first seasons 5-0. After the final gun, Cardinal players lined up to visit with their former coach and other members of his staff.

When the Fighting Irish squared off against Pittsburgh on October 12 at Notre Dame Stadium, they were ranked No. 8 by the Associated Press and being hailed as the surprise team of the season. Willingham's stock was rising with every X and O and his preparation and attention to detail were paying dividends weekly. Another outstanding defensive effort (three turnovers, eight sacks) highlighted a 14-6 victory. The defense stepped up again the following week against 18th-ranked Air Force, the nation's top rushing team, in a 21-14 win on the road. But this

Nick Setta (above), who kicked a school record-tying five field goals in the season opener against Maryland, provided a steady leg throughout Notre Dame's 10-3 season.

Cornerback Shane Walton (above) and flanker Omar Jenkins (below) were big-play contributors on opposite sides of the ball.

time the load was shared by an offense that exploded for 447 yards, 335 on the ground.

Next up for the 7-0 and No. 6-ranked Irish: a crucial game against No. 11 Florida State at Tallahassee.

"We compete and that's the name of the game," the typically low-keyed Willingham said as the Fighting Irish prepared for a battle that could make or break their national title aspirations. "It's about playing, and if we are able to come in here and play better than Florida State, then we win."

The Seminoles fell into the now-familiar Notre Dame trap. They tried to rev up their powerful running attack and were held to 93 yards on the ground. Frustrated, they went to the air and found some success, only to commit three costly turnovers overall that the Irish converted into 17 points.

Holiday threw scoring passes of 65 and 16 yards to Battle and Omar Jenkins, Grant ran for 94 yards and two touchdowns and Setta kicked a pair of field goals in Notre Dame's impressive 34-24 win—a final score made respectable by two late Florida State TDs. While Irish students and subway alumni nationwide celebrated the school's biggest victory since an upset of then-No. 1 Florida State in 1993, Willingham sensed a dark cloud on the horizon.

"I have mixed emotions about our team right now," he said. "I think we did some great things today and we are very fortunate to win against another very, very good football team. But there are some things we need to clean up a little bit."

Willingham, obviously concerned about overconfidence and lack of focus in future games against weaker opponents, spent the next week trying to bring his No. 4-ranked Irish back to earth. Boston College was next up, the same Eagles who had shocked Notre Dame in 1993 when they kicked a last-second field goal in the regular-season finale to hand the Fighting Irish their first loss and dash their national championship hopes—a week after the Irish had upset No. 1 Florida State.

As if on cue, the Eagles did it again. Notre Dame, one of the nation's top teams in turnover margin, fumbled seven times, losing three, and threw two interceptions, one of which Boston College linebacker Josh Ott returned 71 yards for a second-quarter touchdown. The defense was solid

Notre Dame's 2002 resurgence was sparked by a hard-nosed defense that got big contributions from players like junior nose guard Cedric Hilliard (50).

WARNING
Do not strike an opponent with any part of
this helmet or face mask. This is a violation of
football rules and may cause you to suffer severe
brain or neck injury, including paralysis or death.
Severe brain or neck injury may also occur
accidentally while playing football.
NO HELMET CAN PREVENT ALL SUCH INJURIES.
YOU USE THIS HELMET AT YOUR OWN RISK.

adidas

adidas

enough to keep the Irish in the game, but the trademark big plays were missing in a 14-7 loss—the first in Willingham's Notre Dame coaching career.

Green jerseys, 80,935 roaring fans at Notre Dame Stadium, the lure of a possible BCS bowl bid—nothing could rouse the Fighting Irish offense (ranked 109th in Division I-A) out of its slumber on this day. And the lethargy carried over to a game against 1-7 Navy on November 9 in Baltimore, a 30-23 victory that was not secured until Holiday unleashed a 67-yard touchdown pass to Jenkins with 2:08 remaining.

The Fighting Irish seemed to regain lost momentum November 23 when they pounded Rutgers, 42-0, at home and lifted their record to 10-1—Notre Dame's first 10-win season since 1993. But that would be the last win of 2002.

First, USC quarterback Carson Palmer shredded the previously outstanding Notre Dame secondary for 425 yards and four touchdowns in the sixth-ranked Trojans' 44-13 regular season-ending victory at Los Angeles. Then No. 17 North Carolina State bottled the Fighting Irish mystique for one long afternoon and posted a 28-6 victory in the New Year's Day Gator Bowl classic at Jacksonville, Fla. The 2002 season, once colored with optimism, ended on a dreary note—but with everyone clinging to the promise of a bright future under Willingham.

"It's still a very good season," Willingham told reporters after the bowl loss had dropped the Fighting Irish to 10-3 and No. 17 in both major polls. "There are not that many 10-win teams in the country. At the same time, we have to become accustomed to winning our last game, whether it's the regular season or a bowl game."

With Willingham calling the shots, that figures to happen before very long. White sees many of the

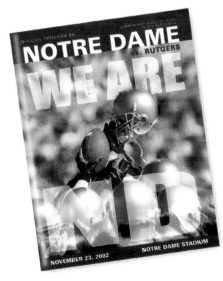

Rutgers was victim No. 10 for the Irish, who lost the season finale to USC and the Gator Bowl to North Carolina State.

same qualities in his coach that previous administrators saw in Rockne, Leahy, Parseghian and Holtz.

"To the people at the NCAA," he said at Willingham's introductory press conference, "he's a man of impeccable integrity. To the recruiting gurus, he's among the very best at attracting talent even when maintaining the highest SAT scores in the nation. He's a disciplinarian whose players love him. He left one of the great universities and one of the great athletic programs in this country to be part of Notre Dame."

Notre Dame's 2002 success raised warning flags in the college football world and Willingham's stock in the national media.

TRADITIONS

TRADITIONS

Alumni revel in the tradi-tion and observers mar-vel at the mystique. To students, it is pride; to first-time visitors a championship aura that perme-ates the South Bend campus on a typical autumn Saturday. No matter the perspective, Notre Dame football shakes down the thunder, wakes up the echoes and stirs up the emotions like a well-scripted passion play.

It also crawls under your skin, an unscratchable itch triggered overtly by any one of numerous campus landmarks, or more

subtly by an inescapable sense of legendary and momentous accomplishment. Images come at you from every direction—subliminal messages and physical reminders as well as the pageantry of football weekends.

"The tradition goes on forever and ever," says former quarterback Terry Hanratty, who helped the Fighting Irish notch one of their 11 national championships in a memorable 1966 season. "I'm sure (Knute) Rockne never dreamed what he was creating. Notre Dame is a special place."

It's special because of such visual triggers as the Golden Dome, Touchdown Jesus, Fair Catch Corby and Notre Dame Stadium, the setting for some of the most incredible football

miracles known to man. This is a tight-knit little campus where fans traditionally have gathered outside the Basilica of the Sacred Heart to greet football players after their game-day Mass and lighted candles at the Grotto alongside such generational regulars as Johnny Lujack and Lou Holtz.

It's also special for students who typically immerse themselves in the football lore they experience every day; for the alumni who flock to South Bend as part of the seasonal football migration, and for the players who get an up-close-and-personal inside look at the Notre Dame mystique. The emotional bombardment is inevitable and thorough.

The shiny golden helmets, a packed Notre Dame Stadium, the atmosphere of game day—tradition is, and always will be, a driving force behind the incredible success of Fighting Irish football.

THE FOUR HORSEMEN, a centerpiece of Notre Dame's storied history, were really four undersized backfield stars who caught the eye and fancy of New York Herald Tribune sportswriter Grantland Rice during an October 18, 1924, Fighting Irish victory over Army. Fullback Elmer Layden (6-0, 162) ran for 60 yards and a touchdown, halfback Jim Crowley (5-11, 162) ran for 102 yards and a TD, halfback Don Miller (5-11, 160) rushed for 148 yards and quarterback Harry Stuhldreher (5-7, 151) completed 2-of-3 passes for 39 yards in a rousing 13-7 win. Rice was so inspired that he began his game story with the immortal words, "Outlined against a blue-gray October sky, the Four Horsemen rode again. In dramatic lore, they are known as Famine, Pestilence, Destruction and Death. Their real names are Stuhldreher, Miller, Crowley and Layden. ..." Eight decades later, the Horsemen are still riding, spiritual reminders of Notre Dame's ever-sustaining football legacy.

The Four Horseman backfield, with Harry Stuhldreher at quarterback and (left to right) Don Miller, Elmer Layden and Jim Crowley, sets up behind a line featuring (left to right) Rip Miller, Noble Kizer, Adam Walsh, John Weibel, Joe Bach and Chuck Collins.

GEORGE GIPP, Notre Dame's career rushing leader for almost 60 years, was a 1920 consensus All-American halfback who died late that year after complications from a strep throat. From his deathbed, with Rockne at his side, Gipp reportedly told his coach, "Some time, Rock, when things are wrong and the breaks are beating the boys, tell them to go in there with all they've got and win just one for the Gipper." Whether Gipp really uttered those oft-quoted words or Rockne simply seized upon an ingenious psychological ploy to inspire his team, there's no doubt the Gipper speech has withstood the test of time. A few writers maintained Rockne used it more than once; most others agreed he used it to inspire his players either before or at halftime of a 1928 upset victory over Army. No matter the details, George Gipp is reverently cemented in Notre Dame lore and Fighting Irish teams are, indeed, still winning "one for the Gipper."

Call it corny, hokey or outdated, but don't underestimate the importance of **"KNUTE ROCKNE, ALL AMERICAN"**—the 1940 movie biography of Notre Dame's legendary coach. Pat O'Brien caught the spirit of Rockne with a rousing performance and the Gipp legend was perpetuated, unforgettably, by actor Ronald Reagan, who would go on to a different kind of distinction. The movie might fall short of must-see status for Notre Dame students, but few will leave the university without an intimate knowledge of its spirited message.

Notre Dame's football aura even translates to the big screen, thanks to Knute Rockne and an unlikely walk-on named Rudy.

To family and friends, he's **DANIEL RUETTIGER.** To millions of fans and movie viewers, he's Rudy, the irrepressible, grimly determined football dreamer who became a real-life symbol of Notre Dame's fighting spirit. Ruettiger, a Holy Cross Junior College transfer who overcame all odds as an undersized Fighting Irish walk-on, was immortalized in a 1993 movie that was filmed primarily on the Notre Dame campus. The popular and inspirational senior realized his lifelong dream of playing for Notre Dame in the final 27 seconds of the 1975 home finale against Georgia Tech, after which he was carried off the field by teammates. Rudy has become a modern-day folk hero.

The Fighting Irish have captured **11 NATIONAL CHAMPIONSHIPS** and produced **SEVEN HEISMAN TROPHY WINNERS**—more than any other Division I university. Success breeds pride, feelings of superiority and expectations, some unrealistic but nevertheless an important thread in the Notre Dame fabric.

John Lattner is one of seven Irish players to win the Heisman Trophy.

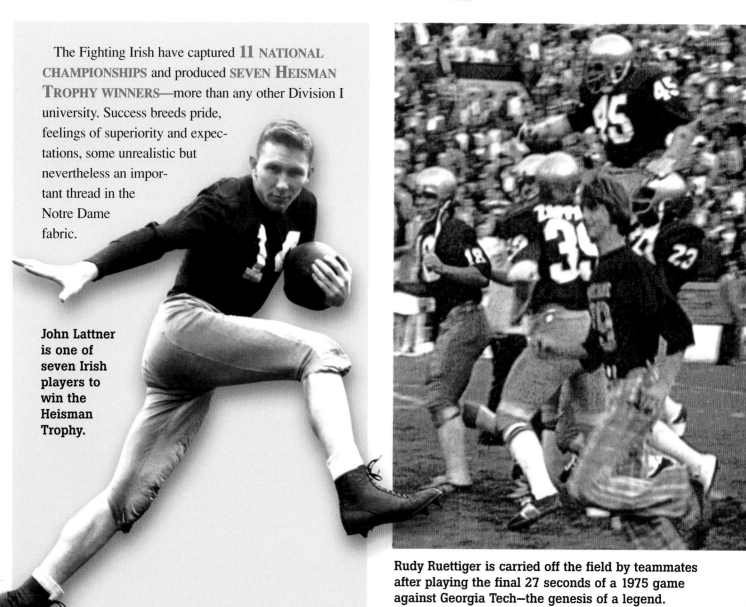

Rudy Ruettiger is carried off the field by teammates after playing the final 27 seconds of a 1975 game against Georgia Tech—the genesis of a legend.

They are **HELMET PAINTERS,** 21 student managers who execute a sacred rite of Notre Dame football. On early Friday afternoons before every home football game—Thursdays before a Saturday road contest—the dedicated juniors gather in the bowels of Notre Dame Stadium and begin the arduous practice of preparing the head pieces for honorable battle. It's a season-long responsibility that is not taken lightly. "The helmets have to be perfect," said Ellen Fitzgerald, a helmet painter during the 2002 season. "I can't stress the word 'perfection' enough. We all love Notre Dame football and we take a lot of pride in what we do."

Tarps have to be spread, tools assembled and more than 100 helmets gathered in what becomes an all-day work party, complete with blaring music, pizza, chats with interested passers-by and friendly banter. All helmets are sanded down and paint thinner is applied by fingers, over and over, until the surfaces are perfectly smooth. Two coats of spray paint precede a final coat that contains actual gold dust. If anything goes wrong with a helmet during the process, the worker redoes it from scratch. Work sessions can go into the wee hours of the morning, although work time usually dwindles as a season progresses and the workers figure out a routine. "We have fun doing it," Fitzgerald said. "We're all really close friends, but we're also very serious about the work."

The test comes on Saturday afternoon when a packed Notre Dame Stadium crowd reacts to its first sighting of the shiny "Golden Domes." "We're very picky about the final looks," Fitzgerald said. "There's no greater rush than to see a player pop out of the tunnel wearing a helmet you painted. You have to make sure it looks the way it should."

Helmet painting is a game week tradition, carried out by 21 dedicated student managers who live by Notre Dame's golden rule.

THE BAND OF THE FIGHTING IRISH, more than 300 members strong, provides the centerpiece for football weekends. It is the oldest university band in continuous existence, dating to 1845, and it has played at every home game since football started in 1887. The band was among the first to include pageantry, precision drills and picture formations. It typically provides a spirited backdrop for the traditional Friday night pep rally and energizes fans and students with a spirited Saturday morning wakeup march through campus and a rousing pregame concert.

The Fighting Irish band provides background music and pageantry for always festive football weekends.

For most students, the FRIDAY NIGHT PEP RALLY is the starting point of their football weekend—and a loud and raucous preview of coming attractions. The rally before the 1997 rededication of expanded Notre Dame Stadium packed in 35,000 wild and crazy fans. A more typical rally now takes place at the Joyce Athletic and Convocation Center (the JACC), where standing-room crowds gather and late-arriving fans often have to be turned away. The pep rally, which has gained national exposure on ESPN, is an hour-long cascade of emotion-triggering music (the electrifying Victory March and

Loud crowds of green are common at both pep rallies and games.

Alma Mater) and motivational rhetoric. The music is provided by the Band of the Fighting Irish; speeches are delivered with fitting vigor by a special guest, two current players and the Irish coach.

Stories still circulate about the late-1960s guest appearance at a Parseghian-staged rally of balding actor Pat O'Brien, who had played Rockne in the movie three decades earlier. "Go out there and crack 'em, crack 'em, crack 'em, crack 'em," an inspired O'Brien exhorted, ignoring the din of exploding firecrackers. "Fight to live. Fight to win. Win, win, win, win. ..." More recent guests, alums such as Phil Donahue, Regis Philbin and George Wendt, have had a tough act to follow.

The Irish Guard, dressed in plaid kilt and bearskin shako, are big enough to run interference for the Fighting Irish band and skilled enough to perform special precision marching routines.

The 10-person IRISH GUARD provides an air of superiority that fits snugly with the Notre Dame mystique. Guardsmen have to be at least 6-2, able to remain silent for long periods and expert scowlers, all the better to intimidate overaggressive fans. They also have to be skilled marchers with a sense of drama and adventure. When properly dressed in plaid Irish kilt and traditional bearskin shako, Guardsmen tower more than 8 feet high. Their primary responsibility is clearing a path, forcefully if necessary, for the Notre Dame band, but they also perform special step maneuvers and formations that have become a big part of every pregame show. "We know they're important, they're protecting us," said Kelly Faehnle, a trumpet player in the band. "Marching doesn't go as smoothly without these huge guys clearing the way. In reality, they're really another section of the band. But their regiment is more strict and they're highly trained precision marchers."

For anyone in need of a game-day charge, the CONCERT ON THE STEPS is a perfect solution. Ninety minutes before kickoff, the band gathers on the steps of Bond Hall and fires up the crowd. "It's so intense on game days; you can really feel the energy," Faehnle said. "The concert is so loud you can feel the ground vibrate beneath you. You look out and see this huge mass of people, especially before the bigger games, and you know they all came to see you." The concert ends with an emotion-tugging rendition of the Alma Mater, after which various sections of the band might perform a spirited mini-show of their own. Properly psyched fans follow the Irish Guard and the band in a lively march to Notre Dame Stadium.

Notre Dame's costumed **LEPRECHAUN MASCOT** is green, active and a game-day presence, whether performing "air pushups" after touchdowns or simply leading cheers. The jut-jawed, two-fisted Leprechaun logo has been officially registered by the university since 1965.

The costumed Leprechaun, one of the most recognizable mascots in college football, is a visible game-day presence and blends in easily with the more traditional cheerleading units.

TIM MCCARTHY, a retired sergeant for the Indiana State Police, has nothing to do with the Notre Dame football program, but he is at the center of a quirky tradition that excites the crowd at every home game. Since 1960, fans have eagerly anticipated his fourth-quarter, pun-enhanced message. When McCarthy

is introduced over the speakers, the stadium grows eerily silent—so quiet you can hear a flask drop. Then McCarthy delivers his message, usually in the form of a bad pun ("Those who have one for the road may have a policeman as a chaser") and the fans explode with touchdown-caliber fury.

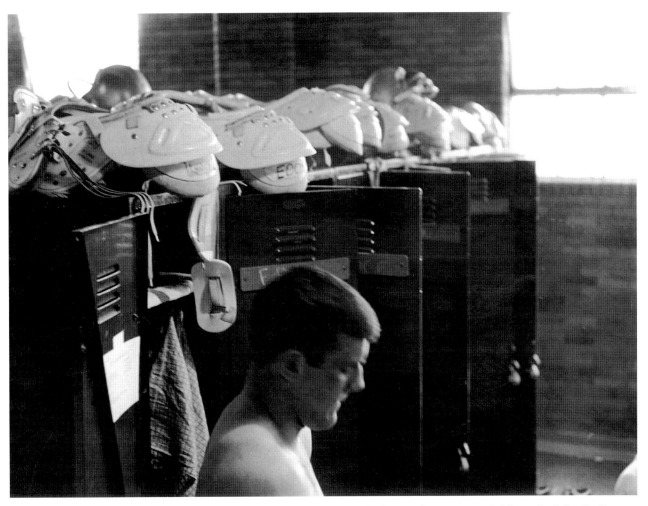

The Notre Dame locker room is hallowed ground—a special place where a special breed of football gladiators have prepared, both physically and emotionally, for battle.

You walk through the double doors and brace for the inevitable rush of emotion. The mystique oozes from every nook and cranny of the **NOTRE DAME LOCKER ROOM,** a place where special players and coaches have prepared for big games, inspirational speeches have been delivered with dramatic flair and tears have been shed, both in absolute joy and gut-wrenching agony. The locker room doubled in size with the 1997 stadium renovation, but care was taken to retain its old-time feel. Walls, rebuilt from original brick, display a plaque with Rockne's famed Gipper speech—a speech delivered before Notre Dame Stadium was even opened in

1930—and tributes to the school's seven Heisman Trophy winners. A trophy case displays Notre Dame's 11 championship rings and tributes to selected former players. But most of all, visitors are overwhelmed by the still-inspirational spirit of Rockne, Leahy, Lujack, Hornung, Hanratty, Theismann, Montana, Zorich and numerous other Fighting Irish legends. "The first time you see it, you know that greatness has been in this room," said Allen Pinkett, an outstanding Irish running back from 1982-85. "You know what's expected of you. You sense this is the real deal, this isn't Podunk U. You know you're expected to win."

From citizen to football warrior—players make the transformation with the touch of an inspirational sign.

1947	9 - 0 - 0
1949	10 - 0 - 0
1966	9 - 0 - 1
1973	11 - 0 - 0
1977	11 - 1 - 0
1988	12 - 0 - 0

PLAY LIKE A CHAMPION TODAY

The players trudge single-file down the narrow steps that lead from the locker room to the tunnel. On the wall, over a landing before the stairs twist in reverse direction, is a gold sign with blue letters that say, "PLAY LIKE A CHAMPION TODAY."

One by one, every player touches the sign for good luck and thus crosses the mental threshold that separates citizen from warrior. The origin of this ritual is a mystery, although it can be traced back at least as far as the Ara Parseghian era in the 1960s.

THE TUNNEL is an important piece of Irish tradition. Physically, it connects the north end zone to the locker-room area below the stands. Emotionally, it connects the fans to the players and the struggle they are about to undertake. In the important 20 or so minutes before every game, this end zone passageway will become the center of Notre Dame's football universe. "It was pretty special the first time I ran out of that tunnel," said Pinkett. "In high school you were used to small crowds, then all of a sudden there's 50,000 screaming fans. It was electric, exciting and intimidating."

The 50,000-plus who crammed into Notre Dame Stadium during Pinkett's era has increased to 80,000 fans, most of whom go into an emotional frenzy when the high-stepping drum major makes a dramatic burst from the tunnel darkness. The drum major is followed closely by the Irish Guard, the crowd-revving band and the gold-helmeted players—an explosive, heart-pumping experience that does not belong exclu-

The dramatic tunnel entrance sends the crowd into a frenzy.

sively to members of the football team.

"When you're in the tunnel for the march-out, the butterflies really start going," said band member Faehnle. "It's hard to describe. You're waiting, you're squished, you're squirming and maybe doing cheers. The band announcer begins his introduction, the drums start and you start jumping up and down. Everybody yells, 'Here we go, yeah!' Suddenly you're trotting. When you emerge from the tunnel onto the field, when you pass the brick wall and are surrounded by photographers, you get a breathless feeling. You're thinking about different things, suddenly there's this wave of noise, you're trying to keep your upper body stiff and count the yard lines—it's crazy. The first time

you do it, you can barely breathe, barely play. It's such a rush coming out of there."

Notre Dame's official colors are blue and gold, but nothing excites the fans—and apparently motivates the players—more than a little green. Knute Rockne used the GREEN GAME-DAY JERSEY as an occasional psychological ploy to fire up the fans and players during his coaching tenure; Frank Leahy used green more often during his reign. But Ara Parseghian made the blue jersey standard from 1964-74, a policy that remained entrenched until Dan Devine's shocking switch to green jerseys before a 1977 USC game at Notre Dame Stadium. The inspired Irish pounded the Trojans, 49-19, that day en route to a national championship and Devine used green jerseys for the rest of the season. Since Devine, the green jersey has been used only occasionally, usually when a coach thinks his team needs that little impromptu shot of adrenaline. "If you think emotion is part of the game, which it is, then those types of things do motivate," said

Joe Montana

Pinkett, who wore green twice under coach Gerry Faust. "But games are usually won with good game plans and execution."

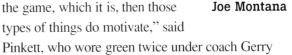

Win or lose, a Notre Dame game ends as it started—with an inspirational tradition. After the final gun sounds, the band plays the fight song one more time as the players file over to the student section and lift their helmets forward in a SALUTE TO THE FANS. Then, after the team has left the field, the band strikes up one more rendition of the Alma Mater as fans lock shoulders, sway back and forth and sing—an out-of-tune but heartfelt tribute to the Fighting Irish spirit so many, from coast to coast and beyond, have come to respect.

NATIONAL CHAMPIONS

NOTRE DAME ~ 1943 ~ NATIONAL CHAMPIONS ~

ZILLY-R.E., ADAMS-R.T. SIGNAIGO-R.G., SZYMANSKI-C. METER-L.G. SULLIVAN-L.T. FLANAGAN-L.E. KELLY-R.H. LEAHY-coach KULBITSKI-F.B. DANCEWICZ-Q., EARLY-L.H. NUMBER TWO TEAM

Bagby Photo Co. South Bend

The Associated Press began crowning collegiate football champions in 1936, the year it introduced its weekly poll of sportswriters and broadcasters. Entering the 1943 season, Notre Dame had failed to win the wire service's coveted mythical national title.

The Heisman Trophy was first awarded in 1935. Entering '43, no Fighting Irish player had won the most prestigious individual award in college football.

Both voids in Notre Dame football lore—the Irish already boasted three pre-AP poll national champs and 22 consensus All-American selections—were filled in 1943, and one honor contributed directly to the other. With quarterback Angelo Bertelli leading the way, Notre Dame was a wire-to-wire leader in the AP rankings.

That Bertelli was around for only six games before reporting for Marine Corps duty mattered little. He set the tone for a remarkable wartime season under the Golden Dome, throwing for 10 touchdowns and helping the Irish to 43.5 points per game before heading for military service at Parris Island, S.C. Bertelli's farewell appearance—against No. 3-rated Navy at Cleveland—cemented Notre Dame's grip on the No. 1 ranking and undoubtedly put him over the top in the Heisman race. Bertelli unleashed three TD passes and ran for a fourth score as the Irish throttled the Midshipmen, 33-6.

Amazingly, a 23-point margin of victory against No. 2-ranked Michigan was the closest call Frank Leahy's team had encountered through its first six games. Powered by five consensus All-Americans—Bertelli, halfback Creighton Miller, end John Yonakor, tackle Jim White and guard/captain Pat Filley—the Irish manhandled the opposition. Miller finished the season with 911 yards rushing, a gaudy figure for that era,

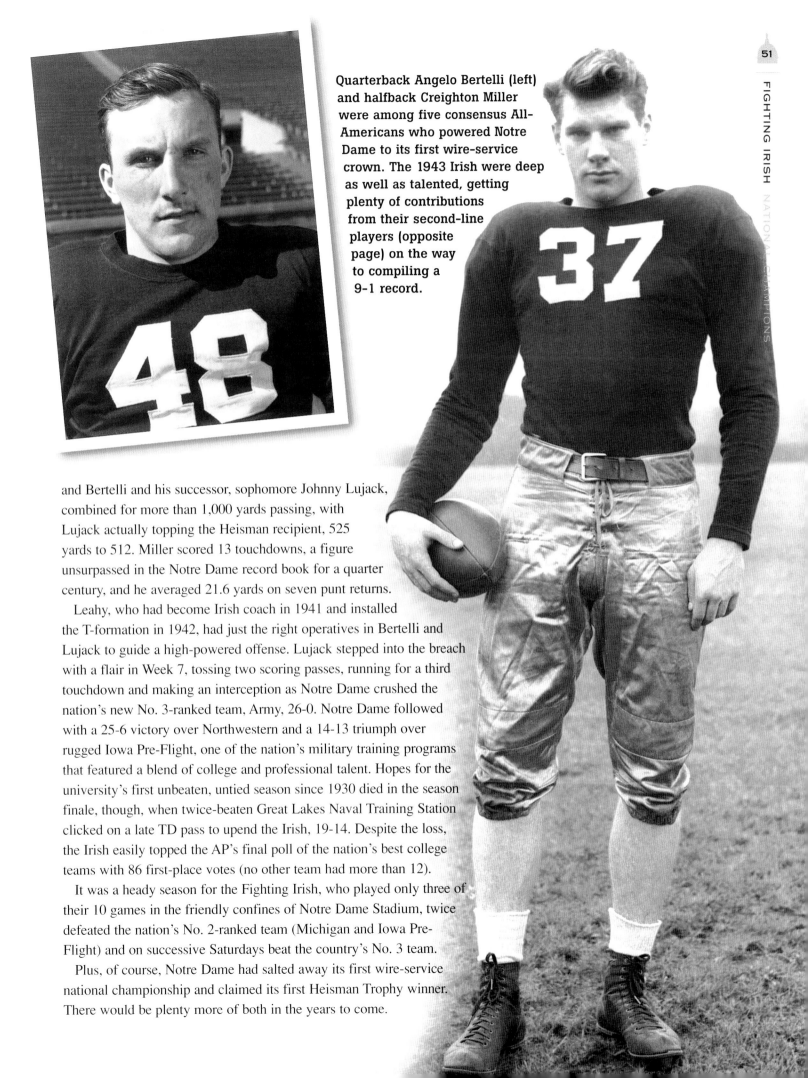

Quarterback Angelo Bertelli (left) and halfback Creighton Miller were among five consensus All-Americans who powered Notre Dame to its first wire-service crown. The 1943 Irish were deep as well as talented, getting plenty of contributions from their second-line players (opposite page) on the way to compiling a 9-1 record.

and Bertelli and his successor, sophomore Johnny Lujack, combined for more than 1,000 yards passing, with Lujack actually topping the Heisman recipient, 525 yards to 512. Miller scored 13 touchdowns, a figure unsurpassed in the Notre Dame record book for a quarter century, and he averaged 21.6 yards on seven punt returns.

Leahy, who had become Irish coach in 1941 and installed the T-formation in 1942, had just the right operatives in Bertelli and Lujack to guide a high-powered offense. Lujack stepped into the breach with a flair in Week 7, tossing two scoring passes, running for a third touchdown and making an interception as Notre Dame crushed the nation's new No. 3-ranked team, Army, 26-0. Notre Dame followed with a 25-6 victory over Northwestern and a 14-13 triumph over rugged Iowa Pre-Flight, one of the nation's military training programs that featured a blend of college and professional talent. Hopes for the university's first unbeaten, untied season since 1930 died in the season finale, though, when twice-beaten Great Lakes Naval Training Station clicked on a late TD pass to upend the Irish, 19-14. Despite the loss, the Irish easily topped the AP's final poll of the nation's best college teams with 86 first-place votes (no other team had more than 12).

It was a heady season for the Fighting Irish, who played only three of their 10 games in the friendly confines of Notre Dame Stadium, twice defeated the nation's No. 2-ranked team (Michigan and Iowa Pre-Flight) and on successive Saturdays beat the country's No. 3 team.

Plus, of course, Notre Dame had salted away its first wire-service national championship and claimed its first Heisman Trophy winner. There would be plenty more of both in the years to come.

Coach Frank Leahy was back in 1946. And so was Notre Dame football.

Leahy had missed the previous two seasons because of service in the U.S. Navy. In his absence, Ed McKeever had coached the Fighting Irish in 1944 and Hugh Devore had directed the team in 1945. The Irish compiled a 15-4-1 record over those two seasons and finished ninth each year in the AP poll. It wasn't exactly a down cycle, but it wasn't Leahy-esque either. The Notre Dame-Army games in those seasons offered compelling evidence the main man wasn't in charge. Army won by the hellacious scores of 59-0 and 48-0.

Jim Martin was a pillar along Notre Dame's line.

The end of World War II brought thousands of Americans back to college campuses—which was especially good news for Notre Dame. Among the returnees to South Bend were Leahy and quarterback Johnny Lujack, who, like Leahy, had spent the 1944 and '45 seasons in the Navy.

Leahy had a deep and talented squad in 1946, one that featured Lujack, Terry Brennan and Emil Sitko in the backfield and such stalwarts as Jim Martin, George Connor, Bill Fischer, Ziggy Czarobski and Jack Zilly along the line. As good as Notre Dame's offense was—and it was methodically efficient—the defense was, in a word, devastating. Five opponents were held scoreless and the other four managed six points each.

Outscoring the opposition by an average of 30.1 points to 2.7, the Fighting Irish rolled to an unbeaten season. But, alas, it was not a perfect season. Army saw to that.

After blitzing its first five foes by a combined 177-18 score, Notre Dame, the nation's No. 2 team, took on the Black Knights of the Hudson on November 9 at Yankee Stadium. Army, led by Glenn Davis and Doc Blanchard, had won 25 consecutive games and was ranked No. 1 in the country. Considering the caliber of offensive talent on the field, a shootout was expected. Instead, the game was filled with big defensive stops and the teams battled to a 0-0 deadlock, an outcome that enabled Army to retain the top spot in the next AP poll and kept the Fighting Irish in the runner-up position.

Notre Dame followed with a 27-0 triumph over Northwestern and then pitched its fourth straight shutout, a 41-0 dismantling of Tulane. Needing help to wrest the No. 1 ranking from Army, the Irish got just that—courtesy of a weak Navy team. The Midshipmen, with only one victory to their credit, played Army tough, losing only 21-18, while the Fighting Irish swept past Southern California, 26-6, in their season finale. Notre Dame's impressive victory and Army's close call prompted poll voters to vault the Irish past the Cadets in the final balloting of the year.

The national championship was Leahy's second in four seasons at Notre Dame. This time, he accomplished the feat with an 8-0-1 team that led the nation in total offense, rushing offense, total defense and scoring defense. Lujack, who excelled on offense all season and made a game-saving, open-field tackle in the Army game, wound up third in the Heisman Trophy voting. Sitko led the Irish in rushing with a modest 346 yards, but he averaged 6.5 yards per carry. And Connor was the recipient of the first-ever Outland Trophy, presented to the nation's best interior lineman.

It was a banner season, if not quite a perfect one. But perfection was not far away for Frank Leahy and the Fighting Irish.

Notre Dame's defense was devastating in 1946 and the Fighting Irish offense, featuring the likes of Emil Sitko (6.5-yard rushing average), was a force, too.

Notre Dame fielded much the same team in 1947 that it did in 1946—and that could mean only good things for coach Frank Leahy and the Fighting Irish faithful.

In fact, the lone major change was a positive one. It involved sophomore Leon Hart, who moved up the depth chart to a starting role at right end. Hart was a ferocious blocker, a talented receiver and a rugged defender.

Hart joined a cast of marquee names that included Johnny Lujack, Emil Sitko, Terry Brennan, George Connor, Ziggy Czarboski and Bill Fischer. Talented and experienced, this was a crew that didn't know the meaning of defeat. No wonder—the '47 Fighting Irish never even fell behind in any of their nine games.

Lujack was the man who made things hap-pen. The Irish quarterback completed 56 percent of his passes, threw for nine touchdowns (at the time, the second-best total in Irish history), gained 11.6 yards per rushing attempt and, on the other side of the ball, led the team in interceptions with three. Sitko paced Notre Dame in rushing yardage for the second consecutive season, running for 426 yards (a 7.1 average). Brennan caught four TD passes and Hart had three receptions for scores.

Notre Dame breezed through its first five games, outscoring Pittsburgh, Purdue, Nebraska, Iowa and Navy, 141-13, in a run that featured shutouts of the Cornhuskers, Hawkeyes and Midshipmen. In the sixth week of the season, the top-ranked Irish took on No. 9 Army, a recent nemesis and a team boasting a 4-1-1 record. Having played the Cadets at New York's Yankee Stadium for 16 consecutive years, Notre Dame got Army at home this time. With more than 59,000 fans on hand at Notre Dame Stadium, the Irish rode the momentum of Brennan's 97-yard kickoff return to a 27-7 triumph.

Northwestern, Tulane and Southern California

Halfback Terry Brennan turned in one of the big plays of the 1947 season for Notre Dame, taking the opening kickoff against Army and sprinting 97 yards to a touchdown. Brennan, a threat as a rusher, returner and receiver, scored 11 TDs overall for an explosive Irish team that also featured the offensive exploits of Johnny Lujack and Emil Sitko.

remained on the schedule. Northwestern put up a surprisingly stiff challenge, losing to Leahy's charges by a 26-19 score. Tulane and USC went meekly, the Green Wave absorbing a 59-6 beating and the Trojans experiencing a 38-7 drubbing.

In the final AP poll of the season, taken in early December, Notre Dame received 107 first-place votes and 1,410 points overall, compared with No. 2 Michigan's 25 first-place ballots and 1,289 points. Trying to prove it was the No. 1 team in the

TALENTED AND EXPERIENCED, THIS WAS A CREW THAT DIDN'T KNOW THE MEANING OF DEFEAT. NO WONDER—THE '47 FIGHTING IRISH NEVER EVEN FELL BEHIND IN ANY OF THEIR NINE GAMES.

land, Michigan figured a rout of USC in the Rose Bowl would support its contention. The unbeaten Wolverines, aiming to top Notre Dame's 31-point victory over the Trojans, overwhelmed the Californians, 49-0, at Pasadena.

With a national debate raging over who was really No. 1, the Associated Press called on sportswriters and broadcasters to vote again in January, and Michigan came out on top this time. Only thing is—much to the consternation of Michigan loyalists—the AP stipulated that the second poll would not change the outcome of the first one. Notre Dame thereby reigned as college football's national champion for the second consecutive year and finished No. 1 for the third time in five seasons.

Notre Dame outpointed Michigan on another front, too. In balloting for the Heisman Trophy, Lujack received 742 votes—187 more than runner-up Bob Chappuis of the Wolverines.

Sophomore Leon Hart showed a knack for hauling in passes, leveling defenders with his blocking skill and delivering big hits on opposing offenses.

Virtually no one gave Notre Dame much of a chance to win the national championship in 1949. And few people expected junior Bob Williams to develop into a first-rate quarterback.

Sure, Notre Dame had gone undefeated for the third consecutive season in 1948 and finished No. 2 (behind Michigan) in the final Associated Press poll. But significant graduation losses—Outland Trophy winner Bill Fischer was among the missing from a 9-0-1 team—and the presence of an unproven quarterback gave the Fighting Irish and their fans cause for pause. Clearly, expectations were lowered in South Bend—even for a team riding a 28-game unbeaten streak (26 wins, zero losses, two ties since the beginning of the 1946 season).

But Williams' emergence, major contributions from veterans Leon Hart and Emil Sitko, a solid showing by halfback Billy Barrett and typically deft coaching by Frank Leahy enabled Notre Dame to charge to the head of the wire-service poll. The Fighting Irish swept through their first nine games in '49—no opponent came closer than 13 points and five lost by more than 30—before running into big trouble in the season finale at Southern Methodist. It took a game-ending interception by Jerry Groom deep in Irish territory to stave off the Mustangs, who were playing without injured star Doak Walker. Notre Dame prevailed, 27-20, completed a 10-0 season and easily outdistanced Bud Wilkinson's Oklahoma Sooners in the final AP rankings.

Williams shattered the single-season Notre Dame record for touchdown passes, throwing for 16 scores. Frank Tripucka, for whom Williams was the backup in 1948, had held the mark with 11. Williams also topped 1,000 yards passing, a feat accomplished only two other times in school history, while making the quantum leap from relative obscurity to consensus All-American.

Hart, a 6-4, 245-pounder, was too much for the opposition to handle. He had five TD receptions from his end position, was a force as a ballcarrier when used strategically at fullback and called signals on defense. His all-around skills made him an easy winner in the Heisman Trophy derby.

Sitko topped the Fighting Irish in rushing yardage for the fourth consecutive season (a feat unparalleled in Notre Dame history) and Barrett, a sophomore, matched Sitko's nine touchdowns. The Irish averaged 36 points and never scored fewer than 27 in one game. And their defense was its usual dominant self, limiting seven opponents to seven or fewer points.

Notre Dame's remarkable run now stretched to four unbeaten seasons and a 36-0-2 record, meaning such players as Sitko, Hart and lineman Jim Martin never tasted defeat in their four years under the Golden Dome. They also had been part of three national-championship teams under the tutelage of Leahy, whose record as Fighting Irish coach now stood at an unfathomable 60-3-5 and included four national titles.

In the pantheon of great sports dynasties, Notre Dame football and coach Frank Leahy had won a special niche. Shaking down the thunder time and again, they set a standard for excellence that few teams on any level could rival.

TED DRAKE

SUCCESSOR TO LUJACK, BERTELLI, RATTERMAN, TRIPUCKA, ETC.

BOB WILLIAMS
NOTRE DAME
QUARTERBACK... 180 POUNDS

HE'S SURE OF GOOD PRESS IN HOME TOWN... HIS BROTHER IS A BALTIMORE NEWSPAPERMAN.

COACH FRANK LEAHY SAYS OF THE BALTIMORE JUNIOR: "BOB WILLIAMS IS DESTINED TO DO GREAT THINGS!"

Fighting Irish coach Frank Leahy saw considerable promise in Jim Mutscheller, who lettered at end for the 1949 national championship squad and then evolved into Notre Dame's go-to receiver over the next two seasons.

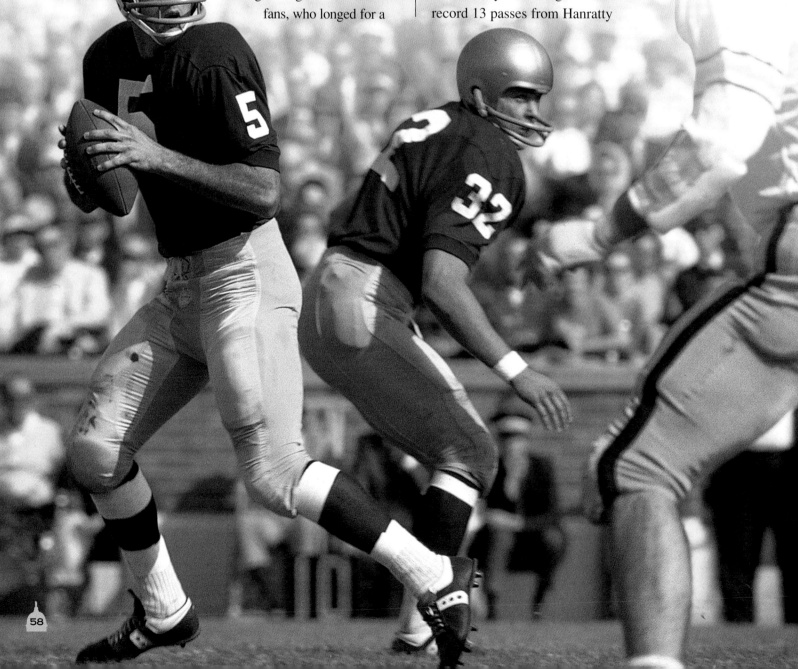

Ara Parseghian had rescued Fighting Irish football from the depths. After the Irish had compiled a very un-Notre Dame-like 19-30 record from 1959 through 1963, Parseghian took over as coach and guided the Irish to a No. 1 ranking entering their last game of the 1964 season. Not even a heartbreaking loss to Southern California in the finale—a defeat that cost Parseghian's team the national championship—could dim the enthusiasm in South Bend.

When the 1966 season dawned, Parseghian owned a 16-3-1 record under the Golden Dome. His outstanding start sent expectations soaring among Notre Dame fans, who longed for a return to the glory days of Rockne and Leahy. Optimism about the '66 season was tempered a bit, though, over the fact the 1965 Irish failed to score a touchdown in their final two games and managed a total of only 20 points in their last three. Notre Dame's passing game had been awful in '65, notching just 85 yards per outing.

Hopes were high that rangy receiver Jim Seymour and one of the new quarterbacks, possibly Terry Hanratty, could inject some firepower into the attack. Seymour didn't disappoint—and Hanratty, a fellow sophomore, stepped up as well. In the '66 season opener against Purdue, Seymour caught a Notre Dame-record 13 passes from Hanratty

With Terry Hanratty sidelined by an injury, Coley O'Brien (3) directed a season-ending 51-0 rout of USC.

for a school-mark 276 yards as the Fighting Irish defeated the Boilermakers, 26-14. Hanratty threw for 304 yards overall.

Notre Dame's offensive juice wasn't confined to its pass-catch tandem. The Irish possessed a gifted stable of backs that included Nick Eddy, Rocky Bleier, Larry Conjar and Bob Gladieux. But as relentless as the offense proved to be—the Irish scored 31 or more points in their next seven games—the defense was even more impressive. Paced by linemen Alan Page and Kevin Hardy, linebackers Jim Lynch and John Pergine and safety Tom Schoen, Notre Dame shut out five opponents (Army, North Carolina, Oklahoma, Pittsburgh and Duke) over a six-week stretch, seized the nation's No. 1 ranking along the way and entered its November 19 showdown against No. 2 Michigan State with an 8-0 record. The Spartans were 9-0 at that juncture.

The Fighting Irish and Duffy Daugherty's Spartans "were outrageously good" in the opinion of Hanratty, who said the 1966 Irish team "was one you only dream about playing for."

The Notre Dame-Michigan State clash—one of many collegiate matchups over the years that would win "Game of the Century" billing—was a rarity in that it

lived up to the hype. In a game played before a capacity crowd in East Lansing, Mich., Notre Dame lost Hanratty to a shoulder separation on a first-quarter draw play (one that Parseghian contended was called by mistake) and trailed, 10-0, in the second quarter before Coley O'Brien, Hanratty's replacement, teamed with Gladieux on a 34-yard scoring pass. The Irish, also playing without the injured Eddy (their No. 1 ballcarrier), pulled even at 10-10 when Joe Azzaro kicked a 28-yard field goal on the first play of the fourth quarter.

The Fighting Irish had additional chances in the late going. With 4:41 to play, Azzaro had an opportunity to send the Irish into the lead but was wide on a 41-yard field-goal attempt. Then, on Notre Dame's final possession, the Irish had a first-and-10 on their own 30 with 1:24 remaining. Surprisingly, the Irish turned conservative and opted for running plays, never moving beyond their own 41. O'Brien did appear ready to throw on one play in the sequence but was nailed for a loss. The game ended in a deadlock.

Parseghian's play-it-cozy strategy at game's end drew plenty of criticism—and the United Press International poll the next week dropped the Irish behind Michigan State. But Notre Dame's ensuing 51-0 annihilation of Southern California convinced both Associated Press and UPI voters that the Fighting Irish were the nation's No. 1 team.

The drought in championships—17 long years—was over.

Quarterback Hanratty (left), getting protection from fullback Larry Conjar, stepped up in his first varsity season and helped the Fighting Irish win their first national title in 17 years.

Lodged in the eighth spot of the Associated Press poll for most of the first half of the 1973 regular season, Notre Dame had little reason to think it could leapfrog seven teams and capture its sixth wire-service national championship.

Still, the Fighting Irish had time—and plenty of talent—on their side.

A 23-14 victory over Southern California in late October—a triumph that ended the Trojans' 23-game unbeaten streak—began to turn more than a few heads. In fact, the win shot the Fighting Irish to No. 5 in the AP rankings.

Five weeks later, after the Irish had thrashed Navy, Pittsburgh, Air Force and Miami (Fla.) to complete a 10-0 regular season, AP voters inched Notre Dame up to the No. 3 slot behind unbeaten and top-ranked Alabama and once-tied Oklahoma.

At this point in poll history, the AP was casting its final ballot *after* the bowl games. Meanwhile, United Press International was in its 24th and last year of releasing its final poll at the conclusion of the regular season. UPI's final balloting for the '73 season decreed that Alabama was the national champion, with Oklahoma listed second, Ohio State third and Notre Dame fourth.

Despite losing out on one poll, the Fighting Irish had more than a fighting chance to claim AP's version of the national title—thanks to a golden opportunity that presented itself when Sugar Bowl officials invited Ara Parseghian's team to take on Paul "Bear" Bryant's Alabama Crimson Tide in the New Orleans postseason classic.

Although Alabama would be favored in the New Year's Eve game, Notre Dame had plenty of weapons at its disposal. Featuring the best running game, statistically, in Fighting Irish history—the '73 team set a school record by rushing for 350.2 yards per game—Notre Dame had averaged 35.8 points during the regular season and scored 44 or more points five times.

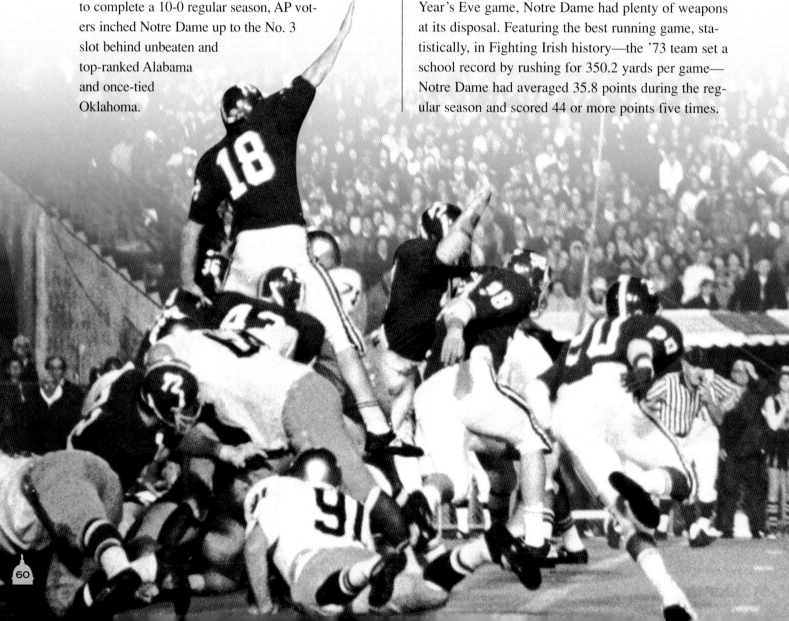

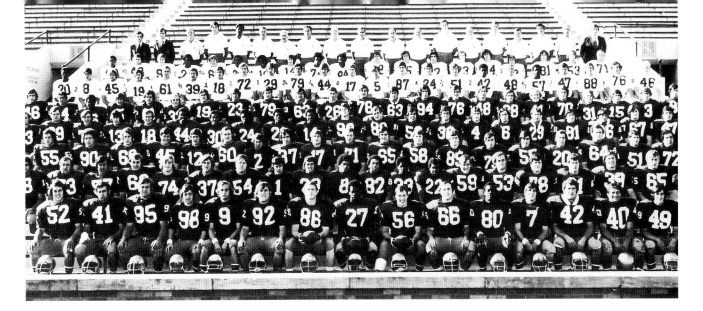

Seldom known for speed in its backfield, Notre Dame had burners in halfbacks Art Best (700 yards) and Eric Penick (586) and a tough, dependable fullback in Wayne Bullock (752 yards). The Irish also boasted an effective passing game, with Tom Clements throwing to such targets as consensus All-American Dave Casper and Pete Demmerle. And the defense, manned by the likes of Ross Browner, Mike Fanning, Greg Collins, Mike Townsend and Luther Bradley, had shut out three opponents and allowed no more than 15 points in any game.

Against Alabama, it was the passing attack that came up big in crucial situations. Clements' 30-yard completion to Casper on third down was the key play in what proved to be Notre Dame's winning drive, a 79-yard, fourth-quarter march capped by Bob Thomas' 19-yard field goal that sent the Irish ahead to stay, 24-23. Later, with the game clock winding down and Notre Dame facing a third-and-eight from its 3-yard line, Clements retreated into his end zone and unloaded a strike to tight end Robin Weber at the Irish 38. The Irish, clinging to their one-point lead, then ran out the clock.

Three days later, the Fighting Irish's ascent to the top became official when AP, in its final poll, named Notre Dame the best team in the nation.

Try as it might, Alabama's stacked-up defense couldn't extend itself high enough to block Bob Thomas' decisive 19-yard field goal in the 1973 Sugar Bowl. The kick came with 4:26 left to play.

Vagas Ferguson takes the ball from Joe Montana and sets sail against Texas in a shocking Irish romp in the Cotton Bowl. Ferguson had a 100-yard, three-TD day.

NATIONAL 1977 CHAMPIONS

The fight for the 1977 national championship turned into a war of attrition. One by one, major-college football's unbeaten teams fell by the wayside—until there was only one, Texas, remaining as the bowl games approached.

There is a belief among poll voters and watchers that if you are going to lose, lose early if you want to entertain any hopes of winning a title. The '77 Fighting Irish took that advice to heart. After opening the season with a 19-9 victory at Pittsburgh, Notre Dame journeyed to Jackson, Miss., where the Irish came out on the short end against the Ole Miss Rebels, 20-13. Unlike teams that suffer defeat in the late going, Notre Dame had more than two months to spruce up its resume— to prove that it was a team on the rise, not one in decline. And week by week, the Irish proceeded to make their case.

With an offense featuring the passing of Joe Montana, the receiving of Ken MacAfee and the running of Jerome Heavens and Vagas Ferguson, and a defense led by Willie Fry, Ross Browner, Bob Golic, Joe Restic and Luther Bradley, the Fighting Irish defeated Purdue, Michigan State and Army ahead of an October 22 date against Southern California at Notre Dame Stadium. Attempting to put a charge into his players and the Notre Dame crowd, Irish coach Dan Devine dressed his team in conventional blue jerseys for pregame warmups but then switched to green jerseys for the game. With the players fired up and the crowd in an uproar as the Irish ran onto the field, USC had the proverbial two chances of winning: slim and none. Notre Dame blitzed the Trojans, 49-19, for its fourth consecutive victory as Montana ran for two touchdowns and passed to tight end MacAfee for two others.

Notre Dame then walloped Navy and Georgia Tech, survived a close call (21-17) at Clemson and rounded out the regular season by pounding Air Force and

Miami (Fla.) by a combined score of 97-10. All of which left Devine's team in the No. 5 slot in both the AP and UPI rankings.

As was the case in 1973 when it was picked to play No. 1 Alabama in the Sugar Bowl, Notre Dame got just the postseason matchup it wanted when the Irish were chosen to play the only still-undefeated team in the country, top-ranked Texas, in the Cotton Bowl. An impressive victory over the Longhorns just might catapult the Irish from fifth to first in the post-bowl polls,

Dan Devine had a lot to smile about in a season that featured his jersey ploy.

a climb that would far surpass the accomplishment of the '73 Irish.

Notre Dame proved to be impressive, all right—to the tune of 38-10. Heavens, who rushed for 994 yards in the regular season (then the second-best total in school history), ran for 101 yards against a shell-shocked Texas team. Ferguson gained 100 yards on the ground and scored three touchdowns (one on a pass from Montana). And the Irish defense, led by Golic's 17 tackles, forced six turnovers.

It was such a dominant performance that voters in the final AP and UPI polls did exactly what the Fighting Irish had in mind—they made Notre Dame the national champion for the seventh time since the introduction of wire-service polling in 1936.

It certainly wasn't the most talented squad Notre Dame ever fielded. Yet the 1988 team was the only one in Notre Dame's storied history to finish 12-0.

The Fighting Irish's No. 1 quarterback was intercepted nearly as often as he threw touchdown passes. A running back did not lead the team in rushing—the quarterback did, which often is an ominous sign. And no Notre Dame player finished with more than 15 receptions. Yet a punishing, opportunistic Irish defense, electrifying special teams and a knack for making the big play more than offset any deficiencies.

Ricky Watters got the season off to a spine-tingling start with an 81-yard punt return for a touchdown against Michigan.

This edition of the Fighting Irish wasn't ranked in the Top 10 when the season began. Yet the Irish maneuvered their way to the No. 1 spot in the polls by early November—and they were still there when the final balloting was conducted after the bowl games.

It all added up to another national championship for Notre Dame. Curiously, the title came in Lou Holtz's third season as Fighting Irish coach—the same span of time it took Frank Leahy, Ara Parseghian and Dan Devine to win national crowns at Notre Dame.

Holtz had preached defense as the key to any success he might enjoy in South Bend, and his '88 team took the message as the gospel truth. It finished the year with the nation's third-best scoring defense, allowing opponents just 12.3 points per game.

In the benchmark game of the season, an October 15 matchup against then-No. 1 Miami (Fla.) at Notre Dame Stadium, the Fighting Irish yielded four touchdowns but forced four Hurricane fumbles, intercepted three passes and upset the Floridians, 31-30. Irish safety Pat Terrell made the game-deciding play, batting away Steve Walsh's two-point conversion pass with 45 seconds remaining. It was the second huge play of the day for Terrell, who had returned an interception 60 yards for a second-quarter touchdown.

Then, with the national championship on the line against No. 3 West Virginia in the Fiesta Bowl, the defense laid a ferocious hit on Mountaineers quarterback Major Harris on the first series of the game. Harris, known for his rollouts and scrambling, suffered a shoulder injury that limited his agility the rest of the night and forced West Virginia to shy away from its trademark option attack. The top-ranked Fighting Irish rolled to a 34-21 triumph.

"The game against West Virginia was no big deal," said tailback/captain Mark Green, who credited the Miami game with giving the Irish a sense of invincibility. "We went into the game (the Fiesta Bowl) totally confident and felt like we were in total control. We wanted to go in there, execute and get out—with the national championship."

Irish quarterback Tony Rice, a strong and elusive runner who in the regular sea-

Pat Terrell's 60-yard interception return for a TD was the first of two huge plays he made against Miami.

son rushed for exactly 700 yards and passed for eight touchdowns (against seven interceptions), ran for a game-high 75 yards against West Virginia and averaged a dazzling 30.4 yards per completion while hitting on seven of 11 pass attempts.

Linebacker Michael Stonebreaker, who combined with tackle Jeff Alm on the jarring stop of Harris, and defensive end Frank Stams won consensus All-American honors for Notre Dame, whose defense also featured the season-long stellar play of tackle Chris Zorich, linebacker Wes Pritchett, cornerback Todd Lyght and Terrell.

Notre Dame's special teams were particularly special in 1988. Raghib "Rocket" Ismail ran back two kickoffs for touchdowns against Rice in Week 9, sprinting 87 and 83 yards. He averaged 36.1 yards on 12 regular-season returns. Ricky Watters spiced a season-opening 19-17 victory over Michigan with an 81-yard punt return for a touchdown, and he bolted 66 yards for a score on a punt runback against Purdue.

The defensive backfield also showed explosiveness when it got its hands on the ball. Besides Terrell's long interception return against Miami, Stonebreaker went 39 yards for a score after an interception against Michigan State and cornerback Stan Smagala picked off a Rodney Peete pass and dashed 64 yards for a touchdown in North Dame's resounding 27-10 victory over Southern California in the regular-season finale.

Additionally, the '88 team received solid contributions from tailbacks Tony Brooks and Green, who often seemed to play in Rice's shadow but rushed for 667 and 646 yards, respectively.

An extremely gifted bunch this Fighting Irish team was not. Worthy national champions the Irish surely were.

Strong and elusive as a runner, Irish quarterback Tony Rice (9) was an efficient-but-not-gifted passer who ran the offense with consummate skill.

For the seasons before 1936, the year in which the Associated Press began its weekly college football poll and thereby put a stamp of legitimacy on the selection of a national champion, the nation's best team was chosen by a consensus of ratings systems in effect at the time and also by the retroactive picks of such organizations as the Los Angeles-based Helms Athletic Foundation.

There is little quibbling about the team deemed the national champion for 1924—the unbeaten, untied, Four Horsemen-led Fighting Irish of Notre Dame.

Coach Knute Rockne was no stranger to perfection, having coached the 1919 and 1920 Notre Dame teams to 9-0 records. But he knew that his '24 team was several cuts above, one that "would always be my favorite team."

The Four Horsemen, made up of quarterback Harry Stuhldreher, fullback Elmer Layden and halfbacks Jim Crowley and Don Miller, drew lofty praise everywhere but none more lyrical than the prose bestowed upon them by *New York Herald Tribune* sportswriter

> ## ROCKNE KNEW THAT HIS '24 TEAM WAS SEVERAL CUTS ABOVE, ONE THAT 'WOULD ALWAYS BE MY FAVORITE TEAM.'

Grantland Rice, whose account of the October 18 Irish-Army game at the Polo Grounds included this passage: "In dramatic lore, they are known as Famine, Pestilence, Destruction and Death. These are only aliases. Their real names are Stuhldreher, Miller, Crowley and Layden." Rice had just watched Stuhldreher deftly run the offense and Miller, Crowley and Layden combine for 310 yards rushing in a 13-7 victory over Army in what would be the Cadets' only loss of the year.

Notre Dame, which boasted a 3-0 record after defeating Army, followed with wins over Princeton, Georgia Tech, Wisconsin, Nebraska, Northwestern and Carnegie Tech. The Horsemen, sprung loose by the blocking of a crafty line known as the Seven Mules, were a force throughout, but so was the defense. Eight of the Fighting Irish's regular-season opponents scored seven or fewer points.

The 9-0 regular season earned the Irish a January 1 date against Ernie Nevers and Stanford in the Rose Bowl. Stanford got 114 yards rushing from Nevers in

NOTRE DAME
National Champions
1924

The Four Horsemen (left to right, Jim Crowley, Elmer Layden, Don Miller and Harry Stuhldreher) left 'Famine, Pestilence, Destruction and Death' in their wake—and outclassed opponents, too.

the big intersectional matchup and dominated the game statistically, but the opportunistic Irish took advantage of Stanford mistakes—the Pacific Coast team turned the ball over eight times— and won, 27-10. Layden scored twice on interception returns, going 78 and 70 yards after picking off passes by Nevers, and end Ed Hunsinger went 20 yards for a touchdown on a fumble-recovery runback. Layden also ran three yards for a TD.

The Four Horsemen, all seniors, didn't go out in a collective blaze of glory at Pasadena, although Layden surely was the game's standout player. But the Horsemen did ride off as the revered standouts of the first national championship team in Notre Dame's proud football history.

The Four Horsemen

By Grantland Rice

POLO GROUNDS, N. Y., Oct. 18, 1924.—Outlined against a blue-gray October sky the Four Horsemen rode again.

In dramatic lore they are known as famine, pestilence, destruction and death. These are only aliases. Their real names are: Stuhldreher, Miller, Crowley and Layden. They formed the crest of the South Bend cyclone before which another fighting Army team was swept over the precipice at the Polo Grounds this afternoon as 55,000 spectators peered down upon the bewildering panorama spread out upon the green plain below.

A cyclone can't be snared. It may be surrounded but somewhere it breaks through to keep on going. When the cyclone starts from South Bend where the candle lights still gleam through the Indiana sycamores those in the way must take to the storm cellars at top speed. The cyclone struck again as Notre Dame beat the Army 13 to 7 with a set of backfield stars that ripped and rushed through a strong Army defense with more speed and power than the warring Cadets could meet.

The outlook for the 1929 season wasn't particularly rosy. The Fighting Irish were coming off a dreary 5-4 season, coach Knute Rockne was suffering from phlebitis and certain to spend a sizable amount of time away from the team and Notre Dame, in the midst of building a 50,000-seat stadium to replace Cartier Field, would play all nine of its games on the road.

Still, Rockne vowed to return Notre Dame football to the level of excellence it had attained before the disappointing '28 season. And, despite turning over many of the coaching duties to top assistant Tom Lieb, he managed to do just that, whether exhorting the team from a wheelchair on the sidelines or talking with his charges via a telephone hookup. Led by versatile quarterback Frank Carideo (a consensus All-American), fullback Joe Savoldi, halfback Jack Elder and a stout defense, the Fighting Irish won at Indiana, edged Navy at Baltimore, upended Wisconsin at Chicago's Soldier Field, prevailed at Carnegie Tech and Georgia Tech and defeated Drake in Chicago. Up next was Southern California.

At this juncture, the Notre Dame-USC rivalry was in its infancy. But the matchup of the Fighting Irish against Howard Jones' powerful Trojans already was a proven gate attraction—120,000 fans had crammed into Soldier Field for their game in 1927. This time, nearly 113,000 fans were on hand for the Irish-Trojans clash, again played at the massive Chicago stadium. With Lieb directing the team, Notre Dame found itself in a 6-6 tie at halftime and in need of some inspirational locker-room oratory. Enter Rockne, whose surprise visit and rah-rah speech—given from a wheelchair—had a telling effect. The Irish seized the lead on a Savoldi touchdown run and got what proved to be the winning margin on Carideo's

extra point in a 13-12 triumph.

After running its record to 8-0 with a 26-6 win at Northwestern, Notre Dame ventured to New York to face Army in the season finale at Yankee Stadium.

Even from a wheelchair, Knute Rockne found a way to inspire his boys in a 1929 game against USC at Chicago's Soldier Field.

The game was played on a raw day on a frozen field at the 6-year-old stadium, and neither team could mount much of an offensive threat. As it turned out, only Notre Dame's Elder found the footing to his liking. He picked off a Cadet pass and traversed 96 yards of icy turf for the only touchdown of the game. Notre Dame made the lead stand up, completing a perfect season with a 7-0 victory.

Although not his usual hands-on self because of illness, Rockne nonetheless made good on his promise to get Notre Dame football back to the top. The consensus of the ratings systems confirmed that he had succeeded—the Fighting Irish were college football's No. 1 team.

There are no degrees of perfection, but somehow the 1930 season seemed more perfect than most for Notre Dame. For one thing, Knute Rockne was hale and hardy, fully recovered from the phlebitis that limited his activity in 1929. For another, the Fighting Irish moved into new Notre Dame Stadium, a striking edifice for which Rockne inspected and approved virtually every piece of mortar. And then there was the team that Rockne prepared to do battle in the showcase stadium—an extremely skilled and deep squad that featured a wealth of backfield talent and an aggressive defense that held all but three opponents to seven or fewer points.

Having Rockne at the helm day in and day out gave an enormous lift to Notre Dame players and fans, the coach's presence clearly intertwined with the mystique of the football program. Rockne was presiding over his 13th Fighting Irish team, and there appeared to be no end in sight to his remarkable achievements.

The Fighting Irish baptized their new stadium with a 20-14 triumph over Southern Methodist, then dedicated it the next week with a 26-2 win over Navy. Victories over Carnegie Tech, Pittsburgh, Indiana, Pennsylvania, Drake and Northwestern followed, leaving Notre Dame with an 8-0 record entering season-ending games against undefeated Army and once-beaten Southern California. All the while, Irish tackle Frank Leahy, lost for the season because of a knee injury, was studying Rockne's every move in hopes of someday carving out a coaching career of his own.

The Army game was contested at the now-familiar football cauldron known as Soldier Field, where the Irish were playing for the sixth time in four years. The weather was nasty—rain, sleet, cold temperatures—and the defenses even nastier. Notre Dame broke through first on a 54-yard run by Marchy Schwartz, who would finish the season with 927 yards rushing (a Fighting Irish record for 46 years). Frank Carideo kicked the extra point, which proved to be decisive when Army made an end-zone recovery of a blocked Irish punt near game's end but failed to convert the point after touchdown. Notre Dame won, 7-6.

The Irish then journeyed to the Los Angeles Coliseum to take on another USC juggernaut. Using fleet second-team halfback Bucky O'Connor to maximum effect at the injury-ravaged fullback position—O'Connor dashed 80 yards for one of his two touchdowns—Rockne masterminded a 27-0 rout of Howard Jones' team, a victory that assured another national title.

It was a glorious moment for Rockne, a coaching giant who at age 43 appeared certain to continue his dominance of the college football landscape for years to come. But fate stepped in, and the cheers turned to tears. Knute Rockne died in a plane crash on March 31, 1931.

Quarterback Frank Carideo was a man of many skills— none more telling than his ability to lead. As a junior in 1929 and a senior in 1930, he guided the Irish to a 19-0 record and two national crowns.

LEGENDARY IRISH TEAMS

1919 George Gipp ran for 729 yards and passed for 727 more as Notre Dame, in its second season under coach Knute Rockne, compiled a 9-0 record. Fighting Irish opponents included the likes of Kalamazoo, Mount Union and Morningside. On October 25, the Irish attracted only 2,500 fans for a home game against Western Michigan, a matchup that Notre Dame won, 53-0.

1920 Gipp rushed for 827 yards in Notre Dame's first seven games but didn't carry the ball against Northwestern in Week 8 because of a shoulder injury and missed the season finale against Michigan State after coming down with a strep throat (the illness which, after complications, led to Gipp's death). The Fighting Irish again finished 9-0. Notre Dame was overwhelming at home, winning its four games in South Bend by a combined score of 136-3.

1927 Notre Dame opened with five victories, then tied Minnesota and lost to Army before winning its final two games against Drake and Southern California. Only Army, which scored an 18-0 victory, dented the Fighting Irish

defense for more than seven points. Christy Flanagan led the 7-1-1 Irish in rushing for the third consecutive season, running for 731 yards.

1938 Needing a victory at Southern California to complete a perfect season, the No. 1-ranked Fighting Irish were upset, 13-0, and finished with an 8-1 record. USC was the only team to score in double figures against Notre Dame. The Fighting Irish drew 55,245 fans, then a Notre Dame Stadium record, for their game against Minnesota, which the Irish won, 19-0. Notre Dame was No. 5 in the final Associated Press poll of sportswriters and broadcasters, balloting that had made its debut in the 1936 season.

1953 Frank Leahy's last Notre Dame team had only one blemish—a 14-14 tie with Iowa in Week 8 that toppled the Fighting Irish from the top spot. The Irish compiled a 9-0-1 mark in John Lattner's Heisman Trophy-winning season and landed in the second spot in both the final AP and United Press polls. (United Press, which would become United Press International in 1958, had begun its rankings in 1950, with coaches doing the balloting.)

John Lattner

1964 Ranked No. 1 in both polls with a 9-0 record, Ara Parseghian's first Fighting Irish team held a 17-0 halftime lead at Southern California in the season finale. Notre Dame wound up losing, 20-17. Irish quarterback John Huarte won the Heisman Trophy in '64, a year in which the Notre Dame defense allowed only 68.7 yards rushing per game, a still-standing school record. Final rankings: No. 3 in both polls.

Heisman winner John Huarte and the Fighting Irish couldn't quite finish off a perfect season in 1964.

Rocky Bleier couldn't help but reflect on the slow start that thwarted the '67 team's national title bid.

1967 Notre Dame, captained by Rocky Bleier, won its final six games to finish 8-2 after losing to Purdue and top-ranked Southern California. A 36-3 victory at Georgia Tech on November 18 was the 500th win in Fighting Irish history. Besides beating up on the Ramblin' Wreck, the Irish also punished California (41-8), Iowa (56-6), Illinois (47-7) and Pittsburgh (38-0). Final rankings: No. 4, UPI; No. 5, AP.

1970 The Joe Theismann-led Fighting Irish took a spotless record into their final regular-season game but were upset by Southern California, 38-28, in Los Angeles. Notre Dame then pulled a shocker of its own, thumping No. 1 Texas, 24-11, in the Cotton Bowl. The 10-1 Irish set school records by averaging 510.5 yards in total offense and 252.7 yards passing. Tom Gatewood set Notre Dame marks with 77 receptions and 1,123 yards receiving. Final rankings: No. 2, AP; No. 5, UPI.

1989 Boasting an 11-0 record entering its last regular-season game, No. 1 Notre Dame came up a 27-10 loser at Miami (Fla.). The Fighting Irish had held the top spot for 12 consecutive weeks. The Irish then toppled Colorado, ranked first in the nation in both polls, by a 21-6 score in the Orange Bowl as Anthony Johnson ran for two touchdowns. Final rankings: No. 2, AP; No. 3, UPI.

1993 In their next-to-last regular-season game, the No. 2 Fighting Irish batted down two late passes by Florida State quarterback Charlie Ward deep in Notre Dame territory and spilled the No. 1 Seminoles, 31-24. Elevated to the No. 1 spot, the 10-0 Irish lost at home to Boston College, 41-39, on a field goal as time expired. Notre Dame then defeated Texas A&M, 24-21, in the Cotton Bowl. Final rankings: No. 2 in both polls (AP and USA Today/CNN, which in 1991 had replaced UPI as the coaches' poll).

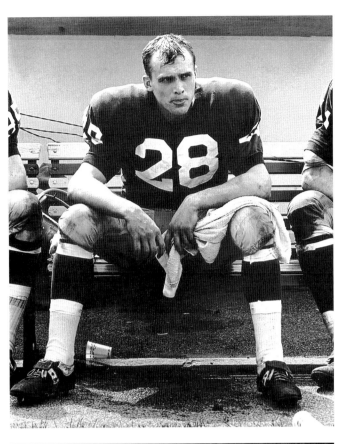

Anthony Johnson scores one of his two Orange Bowl touchdowns for a 1989 Notre Dame team that came oh-so-close to a national championship.

THE COACHES

KNUTE ROCKNE
1918 - 1930

He was a teacher, orator, writer, actor, psychologist, humorist, executive and scientist over an all-too-short 43-year life that ended tragically in a 1931 plane crash. But more than anything else, Knute Rockne was a football coach, by most accounts the greatest in college history, and a pioneer who lifted his sport from regional attraction to national mania. In the process, he created a sports empire and covered a small north-central Indiana university with an impenetrable veil of enchantment.

More than seven decades after his shocking death, Rockne's considerable aura remains interlocked with Notre Dame football. He was part of an unprecedented forward-passing demonstration that put Notre Dame on the national football map in 1913 with a stunning upset of Army. He was the Fighting Irish coach who carved out a 105-12-5 record (a winning percentage of .881, the best in Division I-A history), three national championships and five unbeaten seasons from 1918-30. He was a bigger-than-life personality and coaching innovator whose faster, sleeker offenses redefined the game and filled stadiums throughout the country.

"He had a certain indescribable flame, a physical and mental vitality that few men have possessed," said *New York Herald Tribune* sportswriter Grantland Rice. It was a vitality that fueled a legend and a flame that portended a golden era of football prosperity.

Rockne, born in Norway but raised in Chicago,

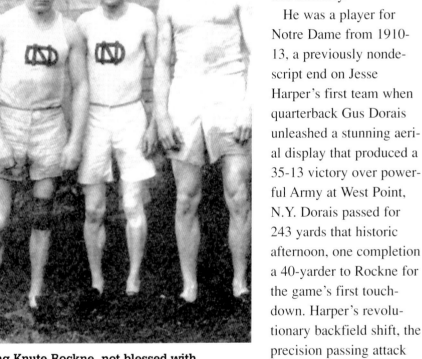

Young Knute Rockne, not blessed with superior athleticism, was a member of the Irish track team (left) as well as a football player.

looked like an "I coulda' been a contender" pug from the poor northwest Logan Square district he called home. He was stocky and prematurely bald, his flattened nose and weathered face giving him a rugged look that camouflaged a quick wit and razor-sharp mind. Not blessed with size or superior athleticism, the 5-8 Rockne earned track and football success through intelligence, determination and intensity.

He was a player for Notre Dame from 1910-13, a previously nondescript end on Jesse Harper's first team when quarterback Gus Dorais unleashed a stunning aerial display that produced a 35-13 victory over powerful Army at West Point, N.Y. Dorais passed for 243 yards that historic afternoon, one completion a 40-yarder to Rockne for the game's first touchdown. Harper's revolutionary backfield shift, the precision passing attack and the balanced offense were concepts Rockne would refine when he became Notre Dame coach five years later.

From respected chemistry teacher and assistant coach under Harper, Rockne quickly rose to championship heights. His 1919 and 1920 teams both finished 9-0, his 1921, '22 and '23 squads a combined 27-3-1. But it was the 1924 Fighting Irish who provided a face for Rockne's growing Notre Dame legend—the 10-0 national champions who were immortalized by Rice's poetic words ("Outlined against a blue-gray October sky, the Four Horsemen rode again. ...") after an impressive win over Army.

Rockne (left) gained coaching acclaim in 1924 when he directed the Fighting Irish and his Four Horsemen backfield to a 10-0 record and national championship.

The poetry was not restricted to Rockne's successful football teams. By 1924, "Rock" had gained national recognition, both as an outstanding coach and a colorful personality. He was sarcastic and soothing, stormy and friendly, humorous and brutally outspoken. Rockne was dynamic, a charming, quick-witted and overpowering presence whether greeting well-wishers after a game or regaling audiences with his after-dinner quips and stories.

"I would have hated to follow him on any banquet program," renowned humorist Will Rogers once said. "He told me many stories and I retold them and got a lot of laughs. If there was anyone I owed royalties to, it was Rock."

Players never quite knew what to expect from their unpredictable coach. Rockne's staccato voice was a practice-field constant, shooting out sarcastic words that deflated egos and withered the strongest of shoulders. His soothing tone and affecting humor were locker-room constants, rebuilding what he had intentionally torn down minutes earlier. He believed in the power of words and was a master psychologist who knew precisely when to chastise or cajole.

Nobody could match Rockne's oratory fervor, which produced inspirational locker-room speeches that were directly responsible for a victory or two per season. Once, after playing a lackluster first half en route to a 10-0 deficit, the players sat quietly in the clubhouse, waiting for the inevitable tirade. But Rockne did not show. The three-minute warning came, but no Rock. Finally, he walked in, looked derisively at his troops and delivered an ego-shattering message: "The Fighting Irish? Well, you'll be able to tell your grandchildren you're the

first Notre Dame team that ever quit." The Irish came back and won that game.

They won another when he directed them onto the field for the second half with the words, "All right, girls, let's go." But Rockne's biggest chill came in 1928 when, midway through a disappointing 5-4 season, he inspired his team by relating the now-immortal 1920 deathbed plea from former Notre Dame star George Gipp.

"When the breaks are beating the boys," former Irish halfback Gipp reportedly told Rockne before dying of pneumonia in a Chicago hospital, "tell them to go in there and win just one for the Gipper." Eight years after Gipp's death, fired up and emotional after listening to Rockne's inspirational story, the Irish broke a scoreless halftime tie and posted a 12-6 win over undefeated Army.

Notre Dame's 1928 taste of mediocrity was sweetened by what followed: powerful 1929 and '30 teams that posted 9-0 and 10-0 records and claimed consecutive national championships. A

Rockne was a multi-layered personality with a big vision.

1930 squad that featured such players as Frank Carideo, Marty Brill, Marchy Schwartz, Bert Metzger, Tom Conley and Tommy Yarr outscored opponents 265-74 and was generally considered Rockne's greatest.

It also was his last. Rockne, en route to Los Angeles to do a promotional film for the Studebaker Corporation he represented, died on March 31, 1931, when the tri-engine plane in which he was flying with seven other passengers crashed in a Kansas wheat field near the small town of Bazaar. News of Rockne's death affected the nation in much the same way President John F. Kennedy's assassination would more than three decades later.

More than 10,000 mourners greeted his casket when it arrived by train at Chicago's Dearborn station and the truck that carried it across town to the LaSalle Street station had to inch its way through packed streets. More than 25,000 greeted the casket's arrival at South Bend and Rockne's funeral, on the day before Easter, was broadcast coast to coast

The ever-resourceful Rockne was not above demonstrating his blocking and tackling techniques to attentive Fighting Irish players on the practice field.

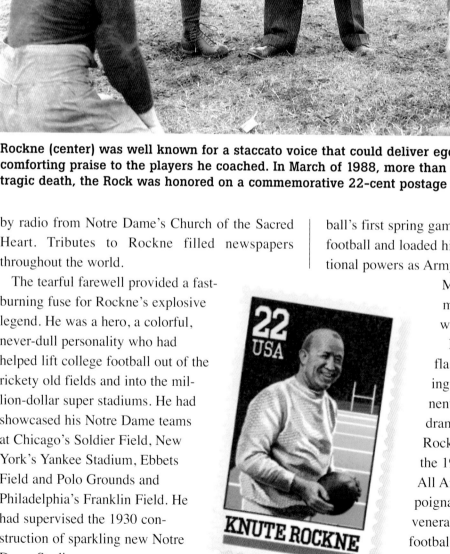

Rockne (center) was well known for a staccato voice that could deliver ego-shattering sarcasm or comforting praise to the players he coached. In March of 1988, more than a half century after his tragic death, the Rock was honored on a commemorative 22-cent postage stamp (below).

by radio from Notre Dame's Church of the Sacred Heart. Tributes to Rockne filled newspapers throughout the world.

The tearful farewell provided a fast-burning fuse for Rockne's explosive legend. He was a hero, a colorful, never-dull personality who had helped lift college football out of the rickety old fields and into the million-dollar super stadiums. He had showcased his Notre Dame teams at Chicago's Soldier Field, New York's Yankee Stadium, Ebbets Field and Polo Grounds and Philadelphia's Franklin Field. He had supervised the 1930 construction of sparkling new Notre Dame Stadium.

It was Rockne who brought speed to the college game, introducing lighter, faster backs who thrived behind his creative shifts. He dabbled with a two-platoon system, used play-action to set up passes, played one of college foot-

22 USA

KNUTE ROCKNE

ball's first spring games, pioneered intersectional football and loaded his schedules with such traditional powers as Army, Navy, Southern Cal, Michigan and Georgia Tech—a major opponent virtually every week.

Rockne's teams were like the flashy boxer jabbing and punching at slower, plodding opponents. And his personality added drama to every encounter.

Rockne's legend was enhanced by the 1940 movie, "Knute Rockne, All American," an outdated but poignant biography that retains a venerable niche in Notre Dame football lore more than six decades later.

The aura that cloaks the most storied program in college football also can be traced to Rockne, an unpretentious Norseman and converted Catholic whose words, deeds and legacy transcend time.

FRANK LEAHY
1941 - 1953

The 87-11-9 record he compiled in 11 seasons at Notre Dame mirrored Knute Rockne's success in the 1920s. And like his former coach and mentor, Frank Leahy was a perfectionist, taskmaster and teacher, dedicated in heart and soul to the perpetuation of Fighting Irish football. But Rockne he was not, and any connection between the two college football giants can be measured more by results and mystique than style and personality.

Leahy, a tackle on Rockne's 1929 national championship team, was a shy, insufferably polite and modest introvert whose cliche-filled speech and stilted verbiage often prompted listeners to question his sincerity. Leahy could be ponderous and humorless, a striking contrast to the robust, witty and dynamic coaching style of Rockne, and was unfairly labeled by some coaches and writers as a phony and hypocrite.

Players who performed on the six unbeaten teams and four national champions Leahy produced from 1941-53, a stint broken by two years of military service during World War II, called him "Sir" to his face and "The Master" in private. They tolerated platitudes that occasionally rang hollow while admiring genius that developed four Heisman Trophy winners, two Outland Trophy recipients, 22 consensus All-Americans and numerous future professionals.

Leahy, the son of a Winner, S.D., policeman, never concerned himself with perceptions, content to immerse himself in that never-ending quest for perfection. "I don't want 99 percent success," he liked to say, "I want 100 percent." It was a goal that consumed him as a student, an athlete and a Rockne protege who would use the information he gained at Notre Dame as the foundation for his coaching career. Rockne, impressed by Leahy's football aptitude, helped him secure an assistant's job at Georgetown and he later served in that role at Michigan State and Fordham.

It was during his tenure as line coach at Fordham that the Seven Blocks of Granite front wall gained national prominence—a line that

Frank Leahy was a two-way tackle for Knute Rockne's 1929 national championship team, an inquisitive observer who fed off the coaching genius of his mentor.

included future National Football League coaching great Vince Lombardi. Two subsequent seasons as head coach at Boston College produced a 20-2 record, his first unblemished mark (11-0 in 1940) and a victory over Tennessee in the 1941 Sugar Bowl, after which Leahy was lured back to South Bend when Elmer Layden (one of Rockne's famed Four Horsemen) resigned after seven seasons and 47 wins as Notre Dame coach.

Leahy quickly displayed his masterful tactical mind, recruiting skills and ability to get the most out of his players, who looked beyond his "sky is falling" speeches and flowery prose to see a coach who was both sincere and blindly dedicated to their well being. Leahy always referred to his players as "lads," addressed them by their formal first name—offensive tackle Bill Fischer was always William; tackle Ziggy Czarobski was Zygmont—and had them perform such character-building tasks as public speaking, charity work and youth coaching.

Sportswriters marveled at such eye-opening Leahy quotes as, "If we win by only one point, I shall be the happiest Irishman in the country." They blanched when, referring to a loaded Irish roster, he told them with straight face, "Notre Dame hopes to field a representative aggregation." Leahy, who constantly expressed unfounded concerns and pessimism about his powerful teams, never understood why anyone would question his sincerity, which friends insisted was genuine.

Leahy's first Irish team posted an 8-0-1 record in 1941 and he produced his first national champion two years later—a 9-1 squad that featured Heisman-winning quarterback Angelo Bertelli. But it was his postwar squads that almost met Leahy's perfectionist goals, posting consecutive 8-0-1, 9-0, 9-0-1 and 10-0 records from 1946-49 while winning three more national titles.

Heisman Trophy winners Johnny Lujack and end Leon Hart, with help from Outland-winning linemen George Connor and Fischer, led the charge for teams that ran up 21 straight wins and a 39-game unbeaten streak while derailing arch-rival Army's mid-1940s championship run. A heralded No. 1-vs.-No. 2 battle between Army and Notre Dame at New York's Yankee Stadium in 1946 resulted in a tense 0-0 tie that ranks among the classic games in football history.

"Notre Dame, under Leahy's leadership,

Leahy's incredible success was the product of hard work, determination and an obsession with winning.

never went in much for weird concoctions or fancy formations," *Baltimore News-Post* sports editor John Steadman wrote in a 1959 retrospective. "The Irish used only the basic stuff, but they employed their plays with machine-like perfection. Leahy could get the full potential from his players and he drilled them incessantly."

A stickler for detail and fundamentals, Leahy was not beyond a little psychology, another trick he picked up from Rockne. When preparing for one strong opponent, he went so far as to regale his skeptical players with stories about terrifying linemen who slept in a forest rather than dormitories. Once, when Czarobski was delivering a less-than-stellar performance, Leahy

Moose Krause (right), who would become a Notre Dame legend in his own right, was a Leahy assistant in 1942.

removed him from the game with the admonition, "Oh, my God, Zygmont, your mother and father are in the stands. You let them down. And you let down Our Lady."

It was not uncommon for the deeply religious Leahy to dig into his Catholic roots and plead with his troops to win one for "Our Lady"—much as Rockne had implored his 1928 team to "win just one for the Gipper." Neither was Leahy above using Rockne as a source of inspiration, occasionally tak-

ing Notre Dame teams to visit his South Bend grave before a big game.

Unlike Rockne's legacy, which was achieved by natural genius, Leahy's was the product of hard work and determination. He drove himself through 18-hour days and asked the players to follow his lead, which they did with minimal complaint. And his 107-13-9 lifetime record, second only to Rockne in Division I-A winning percentage (.864), was achieved against tougher schedules in an era that fostered better coaching and more physical opponents.

Leahy's obsession with work and winning probably kept him from surpassing Rockne's Notre Dame win total. Illness dogged him late in his coaching career and he was sidelined several times during the 1953 season. The final straw came when he collapsed midway through the Fighting Irish's game against Georgia Tech. He led Notre Dame to a 9-0-1 record and No. 2 national ranking that season, watched halfback Johnny Lattner win the Heisman Trophy and then announced his retirement, a shocking blow to Irish football fans. Leahy left at the still-tender age of 45.

He would never coach again, although he kept close tabs on the mystique he helped create. Leahy never wavered in his trust of the Notre Dame system when the Irish struggled through a 2-8 season in 1956, their third year under Terry Brennan.

"I know the material is there," he said. "We can prove it by the number of Notre Dame players signed by the pros. But apparently the coaches haven't been getting through to the boys and impressing them with the deep tradition of Notre Dame football.

"When a player comes to Notre Dame, it is, in most cases, the realization of a dream. He is determined to do

anything to maintain the tradition, and he is a pliable, coachable athlete. At least, I found him that way and I don't think he has changed."

Leahy did serve as the first general manager (1959-60) of the American Football League's Los Angeles Chargers and worked various other jobs to support his wife and eight children. The square-jawed Irishman who produced more national championships than any other Notre Dame coach died in 1973 after battling back problems, leukemia and diabetes.

Leahy's 1946 and '47 national championship teams were built around an all-star cast that included Johnny Lujack (32), George Connor (81), Jim Martin (38) and Leon Hart (82).

Leahy's off-field musings
sometimes rankled writers,
but nobody could criticize his
legendary sideline genius.

ARA PARSEGHIAN
1964 - 1974

He hit South Bend like a bolt of lightning and left Notre Dame 11 years later almost as dramatically. While he was there, Ara Parseghian recharged a sluggish Fighting Irish football program with his high-voltage coaching style, stoked enthusiasm with his electrifying personality and woke up a few echoes with his emotional Knute Rockne- and Frank Leahy-like pursuit of perfection.

Parseghian, the son of an Armenian father and French mother, posted a 95-17-4 record from 1964-74 and led the Irish to two national championships—their first since 1949 under Leahy. In the process, he reversed a 19-30 five-year struggle under the leadership of Joe Kuharich and interim Hugh Devore. But the "Era of Ara" is best defined by his debut season, a 1964 campaign that some rank as the most memorable—and frustrating—in Notre Dame history.

The Irish, coming off a 2-7 record in 1963, hired Akron, Ohio, native Parseghian to replace Devore as the first step in what figured to be a lengthy rebuilding process. He was not Catholic, he had no Notre Dame ties or Irish roots and his 36-35-1 coaching record in eight years at Northwestern suggested an ability to turn around down-and-out programs. He was charming, energetic and confident, qualities that would buy time while a makeover was performed.

Parseghian, however, was not inclined to waste valuable time. He was a superior strategist, the product of two professional seasons as a player under Cleveland's Paul Brown and a half season as Miami of Ohio assistant under Woody Hayes. He was a detail-minded organizer and disciplinarian, qualities he refined in his five-year stint as Hayes' successor at Miami. He was a master of preparation and a fiery competitor. And he was a motivator and

psychologist who could cast a spell over players and fans, vintage Notre Dame legend Rockne.

Parseghian raised eyebrows by turning his 1964 team over to senior quarterback John Huarte, a no-name backup who had yet to earn a letter. Huarte would win the Heisman Trophy. Parseghian converted defensive end Jack Snow (who also had

Detail-minded and always prepared, Ara Parseghian ruled over a colorful period of Notre Dame history.

seen duty at wing-back) into a wide receiver and Huarte's go-to target. He became a consensus All-American. Parseghian instilled confidence in his team, inspired players with his motivational ploys and watched a little old-fashioned Irish magic unfold.

"He taught us pride, all right," said Jim Carroll, an offensive guard and Parseghian's first captain. "And he showed us confidence."

The Irish won at Wisconsin to open the season and upset Purdue, 34-15, at Notre Dame Stadium. Shockingly, the Irish continued to win, stretching their record to 9-0 and earning the No. 1 ranking in both wire-service polls

Ever the motivator and psychologist, Parseghian cast a spell over fans and players while coaching the Fighting Irish to two national championships.

of lowering the gates and letting anyone in who could play football. We might have been criticized if, say, we had been 3-7 that first year and maybe 5-5 the second."

There would be no 3-7 or 5-5 records in Parseghian's Notre Dame tenure. A 7-2-1 mark in 1965 preceded the Fighting Irish's 9-0-1 run to a national championship in 1966; an 8-3 performance in 1972 foreshadowed a perfect 11-0 title-winning romp in 1973. That was as bad, and as good, as it got in a golden era of football.

Those close to the Notre Dame program marveled at Parseghian's upbeat coaching techniques and organization. Practices were planned to the smallest detail

heading into their season finale at Southern Cal. The unthinkable, a national championship in Parseghian's first season, was only 30 minutes away from reality when the Fighting Irish entered their locker room at halftime with a 17-0 advantage over the Trojans.

But the magic suddenly wore off. USC scored a touchdown in the third quarter and another with just over 5 minutes remaining in the game. Craig Fertig's 15-yard TD pass to Rod Sherman with 1:33 to go gave Southern Cal a championship-denying 20-17 victory. Notre Dame, which finished third in the final polls, had a fourth-quarter touchdown wiped out by a holding penalty. But nothing could wipe out that blue-and-gold feeling of accomplishment.

"I'm glad we went 9-1 that first season," Parseghian said later. "We did it with the players that were already there and nobody could accuse us

and the coach was always in the middle of the action. It was not uncommon to see the handsome 190-pound Parseghian leading calisthenics, running pass patterns, trading blows with defensive linemen and bumping with cornerbacks and safeties. His charismatic one-of-the-guys enthusiasm was contagious.

It also was hard to escape his blitz of slogans ("The difference between mediocrity and greatness is a little extra effort!") and motivational jabs. The discipline he demanded from his players was mirrored by a rigid personal routine that began at 5:30 every morning and seldom ended until late at night. He worked his players hard early in the week and gradually transferred his emphasis from physical to mental as game day approached.

Not even Parseghian could have been mentally prepared for the decision that faced him in a 1966 game against Michigan State—a much-celebrated

Star receiver Jim Seymour (85) was a Parseghian weapon during Notre Dame's 1966 title season.

No. 1-vs.-No. 2 battle of unbeatens at East Lansing, Mich. The 8-0 Irish were top ranked in both wire-service polls; the 9-0 Spartans were second in both. When Parseghian's Irish ran out the clock to preserve a 10-10 tie instead of going for a victory (thus enhancing the No. 1 ranking in his mind), he became an easy target for critics. But in the end, Notre Dame claimed the national title.

There was no such criticism in 1973. Led by quarterback Tom Clements, tight end Dave Casper and defensive end Ross Browner, the Irish outscored opponents 358-66 in the regular season en route to a 10-0 record. They secured another national championship with a pulsating 24-23 Sugar Bowl win over top-ranked Alabama, a game decided by Bob Thomas' 19-yard field goal with 4:26 remaining.

Parseghian, emotionally drained and dogged by health problems stemming from the most pressure-filled job in college football, resigned with a 170-58-6 career record after leading the Irish to a 13-11 victory over Alabama in the 1975 Orange Bowl, completing a 10-2 final season. That gave him wins in three of the big four bowls—the Cotton, Sugar and Orange—after Notre Dame ended its 45-year policy of not playing postseason games in 1969.

Parseghian, whose only post-Irish association with football came as an analyst and commentator for ABC Sports and CBS Sports, produced 21 consensus All-Americans, almost two per season.

Parseghian was a teacher and master strategist, qualities not lost on players like 1968 split end Tom Eaton (89).

DAN DEVINE
1975 - 1980

ing successfully on the winning legacy of his predecessor.

Replacing a legend was nothing new for Devine, who jump-started his coaching career with a 27-3-1 record at Arizona State from 1955-57. He moved to Missouri in 1958, one season removed from the retirement of Tigers guru Don Faurot, and posted a 93-37-7 mark through 1970. His four-year stint (25-28-4 from 1971-74) as coach and general manager of the National Football League's Green Bay Packers was spent in the still-looming shadow of Vince Lombardi.

At Notre Dame, Devine inherited Parseghian's well-stocked roster and produced 8-3 and 9-3 records in 1975 and '76. But it was his 1977 team, featuring quarterback Joe Montana, halfback Vagas Ferguson and defensive stars Ross Browner, Bob Golic and Luther Bradley, that silenced skeptics who questioned his low-key approach.

The Fighting Irish lost to Mississippi in the second game of the season but rolled through the remainder of their schedule, securing the national championship with a rousing 38-10 Cotton Bowl victory over previously top-ranked Texas.

"It's a shame he had to go through so much his first two years here," middle guard Golic told the *Dallas Morning News* prior to the 1978 Cotton Bowl. "He was not given a chance. People still had Ara on their minds. Coach Devine has his spurts where he does get outspoken, but before the game he doesn't say anything more or anything less than he has to."

Stories circulated about Devine's inflexibility with players and obsession for detail and neatness. Players shrugged off the rumors. They talked about his well-organized practices, unbiased personnel decisions, situational motivation ploys and detailed preparation for games. He did have his quirks, such as a penchant for soaking his whistle in alcohol before practice and an obsessive desire to tidy his office during meetings and interviews. But players also saw the caring side of Devine, a

By most standards, it was an outstanding six-season stretch that produced 53 wins, three bowl victories and a national championship. But success is measured differently at Notre Dame, where Dan Devine, a quiet and quirky Irish Catholic, never managed to satisfy the game's most demanding alumni and fans. Call it a classic case of bad timing.

Devine's greatest sin was not being Ara Parseghian, the fiery, charismatic savior who returned Notre Dame to college football's Promised Land from 1964-74. Irish fans loved the volatile, hard-charging style of Parseghian; they never bought in to the private, soft-spoken and cautious ways of Devine, even while he was build-

father of seven children and a devout Catholic.

"You don't waste any time here," Ferguson said, referring to Devine's emphasis on detail. "Everything is planned out and timed to the minute. That's the biggest difference I've found between high school ball and here. We get so much more out of our time here."

Devine followed his 1977 championship with 9-3, 7-4 and 9-2-1 records that lifted his Notre Dame ledger to 53-16-1, a .764 winning percentage that compared favorably with such former Irish

coaching heavyweights as Knute Rockne, Frank Leahy and Parseghian. Victories in the 1976 Gator Bowl and the 1978 and '79 Cotton Bowls built on the postseason success of Parseghian.

Devine resigned after the 1980 season with a career coaching mark of 173-56-9 and returned to his college football roots as executive director of the Arizona State Sun Angel Foundation in Phoenix. He later worked as athletic director at Missouri. Devine died in May 2002.

Dan Devine had a softer, less-volatile style than predecessor Parseghian, but he guided quarterback Joe Montana (below) and the 1977 Irish to a national title.

LOU HOLTZ
1986 - 1996

Fast-talking, quick-quipping Lou Holtz reached championship heights in 1988, his third season as coach of the Fighting Irish.

Behind his fast-talking, quick-quipping veneer beat the heart of a lion. Anybody who accepted Lou Holtz on face value seriously underestimated one of the game's most intense, driven, demanding, creative and organized football minds. Comedian, entertainer, coach and amateur magician—the captivating little man with the thick glasses made Notre Dame's football mystique reappear.

To Fighting Irish fans with long memories, Holtz was a reincarnation of Knute Rockne. He could mesmerize audiences with his one-liners and humorous stories while spreading the gospel of Notre Dame football with energy and enthusiasm. Neither Rockne nor Holtz ever met a hard-core Fighting Irish fan he could not charm. Both were

tough disciplinarians, innovative strategists and masterful motivators and recruiters.

"When we first hired him (in 1986), a guy from Chicago said to me, 'How can you hire a guy to coach your football team who's a quipster?' " said Gene Corrigan, Notre Dame's former athletic director. "And I said, 'Have you read anything about Rockne? He's the greatest one-liner guy of all time.' Lou is very much like him. He's the kind of guy who can wake up the echoes."

That was important to a Notre Dame program that had stumbled through a five-year period of mediocrity under Gerry Faust. When Holtz arrived, fans and alumni who had come to expect football success were testy, impatient and unwilling to accept anything short of excellence.

"We had to have someone of impeccable integrity and character," the Rev. Edmund Joyce, overseer of Notre Dame's athletic department for 35 years, told *The Sporting News* in 1988. "We have never told any coach he had to win a national title or win this many games. We just tell them to be honest and live within our rules."

Holtz, working with a thin roster inherited from Faust in 1986, guided his first team to a 5-6 record. Former Irish coach Ara Parseghian watched Holtz work and predicted he would return the Irish to championship contention in three years. It didn't take that long.

Holtz's second team, featuring Heisman Trophy-winning receiver Tim Brown, finished 8-4, losing to Texas A&M in the Cotton Bowl. The 1988 Fighting Irish, loaded with underclassmen, stormed to 11 straight regular-season wins, a convincing 34-21 win over West Virginia in the Fiesta Bowl and the school's first national championship since 1977. Like Frank Leahy, Parseghian and Dan Devine before him, Holtz had produced a title in his third Notre Dame season.

The 1989 Irish almost gave Holtz something that only Rockne and Leahy had accomplished—back-to-back national championships. A team featuring 1988 holdovers Tony Rice (quarterback), Ricky Watters (running back), Raghib Ismail (flanker), Tim Grunhard (guard), Chris Zorich (nose tackle) and Todd Lyght (cornerback) rolled to an 11-0 record and No. 1 ranking before losing in the regular-season finale to the Miami Hurricanes. Not even a 21-6 Orange Bowl win over top-ranked Colorado could salvage the Irish's championship hopes.

Holtz's 1992 team finished 10-1-1 and his '93 squad saw another bid for an undefeated season and national championship end in the regular-season finale with a 41-39 upset loss to Boston College. The Holtz magic lasted through 1996, when the proud Ohioan retired with a 100-30-2 Notre Dame record, a 216-95-7 overall mark that included stints at William & Mary, North Carolina State, Arkansas and Minnesota. Five of his 11 Irish teams finished sixth or higher in the final Associated Press polls and nine played in New Year's bowl games.

After working for CBS Sports as an analyst for two years, Holtz returned to the football wars in 1999 as head coach at South Carolina.

Holtz was always colorful, whether leading the Fighting Irish into battle (below left), exhorting them to victory (center) or contemplating his next move, which typically was a good one.

OTHER COACHES

It is the most time-eating, health-sapping, pressure-packed job in college football. It's also the opportunity of a lifetime, a bittersweet top-of-the-profession brush with destiny. The head coaching job at Notre Dame is empowering and humbling, rewarding and frustrating—a career-defining challenge tinged with impatience and high expectations.

Knute Rockne set the bar so high in the 1920s that few coaches have been able to touch his near-perfect blend of coaching ability, success and charm. Rockne almost single-handedly turned a small, north-central Indiana university into a national football power, created an aura that has endured the test of time and established a winning tradition that defies explanation.

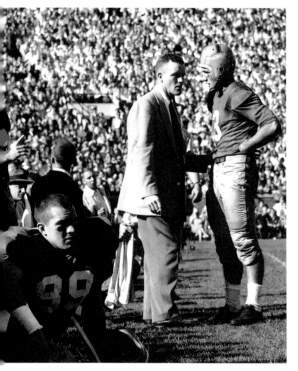

Former Irish halfback Terry Brennan (wearing suit) lasted five seasons in the Notre Dame hot seat.

"I went to Notre Dame hoping all my expectations would be fulfilled," Lou Holtz told reporters when he was hired in 1986, "and it's been even more than I envisioned. It's the mystique. You can sense it and feel it, but you can't describe it."

Holtz, who compiled a 100-30-2 record in 11 seasons and produced the school's most recent national championship, is one of the few who survived the mystique. Frank Leahy, with his four national titles and .855 winning percentage, reinforced Rockne's legacy and inched the Notre Dame coaching bar a little higher. So did the charismatic and successful Ara Parseghian

Ed McKeever stepped out of Frank Leahy's shadow to guide the 1944 Irish to an 8-2 record.

from 1964-74. Success at Notre Dame is measured by different standards than anywhere else.

Former Rockne player and assistant Hunk Anderson was the first to find that out in 1931 when he replaced the Rock, compiled a 16-9-2 record and was gone after three seasons. Elmer Layden, one of Rockne's famed Four Horsemen, compiled a sparkling 47-13-3 mark over seven seasons but never produced a national championship. Terry Brennan had the unpleasant task of following Leahy in 1954 and was 32-18 over five seasons, a .640 winning percentage that would have been praised at most universities but fell short at South Bend.

"Gerry Faust (30-26-1 from 1981-

Gerry Faust was an easy target for critics.

85) would say he was a good coach," former Irish athletic director Gene Corrigan said when Faust was replaced by Holtz in 1986, "but you have to be a great coach to be successful here." Faust, the formerly outstanding Moeller High School (Cincinnati) coach, was an easy target for critics in what was generally considered a down period for Notre Dame football.

Qualifications for the Notre Dame job include a thick skin, workaholic energy, charm and wit, motivational ability and the understanding that winning—game after game, season after season—defines success. With the expectations come restrictions. Fighting Irish coaches face restrictive redshirt and transfer policies; there are no athletic dorms; players get no special treatment from the admissions office; players are expected to be students first—and to graduate.

But Notre Dame coaches also know the tradition, the winning aura, attracts the top high school recruits, an advantage few colleges enjoy. That might explain why only one coach in Notre Dame history, Joe Kuharich from 1959-62, compiled a losing record (17-23), and why the five-year stretches under Faust and Bob Davie (35-25) so tortured alumni and fans who were appeased only by "winning revivals"

The Bob Davie years (1997-2001), good enough for many college programs, fell short of Irish expectations.

Hugh Devore, pictured in 1962 with Dick Arrington (63) and Dave Humenik (75), was 9-9-1 as a two-time interim coach.

under Holtz and current coach Tyrone Willingham.

All Notre Dame coaches, however, have at least been given a chance to succeed. Other than interim coaches Ed McKeever and Hugh Devore, only two coaches since Jesse Harper took over in 1913 have lasted fewer than five years—Anderson and Kuharich. McKeever was 8-2 as a one-season replacement in 1944 while Leahy served in the Navy during World War II. Devore was 7-2-1 in 1945 while filling in for Leahy and 2-7 in 1963, the season before Parseghian arrived.

Conversely, no coach since Rockne has remained in the Notre Dame hot seat for more than 11 seasons.

THE
UNFORGETTABLES

ANGELO BERTELLI

Notre Dame coach Frank Leahy called him "the worst runner I've ever coached." And teammates joked about his unorthodox style, feet churning back and forth, almost like a skating motion with little or no knee lift. But there was nothing unorthodox or funny about the golden arm that propelled Angelo Bertelli to Heisman Trophy heights and the Fighting Irish to a 1943 national championship.

Bertelli was like a square peg trying to fit into a round hole when he arrived at South Bend in 1940, fulfilling the Notre Dame dream he had nourished since childhood in Springfield, Mass. He was a 6-1, 175-pound former high school hockey, baseball and football star who commanded attention with his strong, accurate throws and ability to hit targets in full stride.

The quick-strike potential of Bertelli was lost on Irish coach Elmer Layden, who was looking for halfbacks who could run first and pass later in the single-wing Notre Dame box offense that had been used by Irish teams since Knute Rockne. The youngster became buried, hopelessly it seemed, on Layden's depth chart.

But Bertelli's career path would take a dramatic turn. Layden departed to become commissioner of the National Football League, Leahy returned to coach his alma mater and Bertelli, who had been recruited by Leahy when he coached at Boston College, became his halfback—a pass-first star who threw for eight touchdowns and a Notre Dame-record 1,027 yards while helping the Fighting Irish to their first undefeated season (8-0-1) since 1930.

Bertelli, who finished second in the 1941 Heisman voting to Minnesota's Bruce Smith, became a marked man. Leahy knew his run-challenged star would be compromised at halfback by innovative defenses. So he dumped the Rockne box, made the dramatic switch to the revolutionary T-formation and taught Bertelli the intricacies of fakes, spins, footwork and ballhandling while giving his team a better offensive balance.

The 1942 Fighting Irish opened with a tie and loss while adjusting to the new system, but a 7-2-2 final record was more than respectable and Bertelli posted his second straight 1,000-yard season, completing 72-of-159 passes for 1,039 yards and 10 touchdowns. That was an appetizer.

Through the first six games of 1943, Bertelli fired 10 TD passes and directed an offense that averaged 43.5 points while crafting a winning margin of 38.3. The Bertelli-led Fighting Irish carried a No. 1 Associated Press ranking and undefeated record into a Game 6 showdown with No. 3 Navy and blasted the Midshipmen, 33-6. Bertelli was outstanding, passing for three touchdowns and even running for one—but that's where it ended. He was called by the Marine Corps and reported for immediate wartime duty.

The Irish went on to beat No. 3 Army, No. 8 Northwestern and No. 2 Iowa Pre-Flight under the leadership of sophomore quarterback Johnny Lujack. But hopes for an undefeated season went down the drain in the season finale when Great Lakes Naval Station scored a touchdown with 33 seconds remaining to beat Notre Dame, 19-14.

Bertelli, who listened to the devastating loss at his Parris Island, S.C., training camp, was handed a startling telegram minutes later. It told him he had won the Heisman Trophy for his six-game 1943 performance. And a few days later, Notre Dame, despite its season-ending loss, was crowned national champion for the first time in 13 years.

JOHNNY LUJACK

HEISMAN TROPHY 1947

Everything about him smacked of success—the incredible athleticism, the Hollywood good looks, the modest sincerity, the honest, straightforward way he handled celebrity. Even his name ... Johnny Lujack ... rolled off the tongue with lyrical flair.

Such was the mojo of Notre Dame's most storied quarterback that the teams for which he played carved out a sensational 26-1-1 three-year record and won three national championships. Such was the appetite for heroic figures in the wake of World War II that Lujack became a national icon en route to becoming the Fighting Irish's second Heisman Trophy winner in five seasons.

"Lujack's figure completely dominated the football field this fall and the record of the great Notre

Johnny Lujack (32) was a
big weapon for title teams
coached by Frank Leahy.

Dame team is his testimonial," Furman Bisher wrote in the *Charlotte News* after Frank Leahy's Fighting Irish had posted a 9-0 record on their way to the 1947 title. That memorable season followed on the heels of an 8-0-1 title-winning 1946 campaign, another Lujack masterpiece.

Notre Dame's first Heisman winner, quarterback Angelo Bertelli in 1943, also benefited from the Lujack magic. Bertelli, an outstanding passer in Notre Dame's 2-year-old T-formation offense, led the powerful Irish to a 6-0 record before heeding the call of the U.S. Marine Corps. Lujack, a sophomore, stepped in as Bertelli's replacement and led top-ranked Notre Dame to consecutive wins over No. 3 Army, No. 8 Northwestern and No. 2 Iowa Pre-Flight before a stunning season-ending loss to Great Lakes Naval Station. Despite the last-minute shocker—the only loss in Lujack's Notre Dame varsity career—the Irish finished as the nation's No. 1 team.

Lujack missed the 1944 and '45 seasons while serving in the Navy. He returned in 1946, healthy, hungry and ready to expand on his 1943 heroics. Lujack's greatest acclaim was achieved as the heady, poised and clever T-formation signal-caller for some of the most talented teams ever assembled. But he also was a punter and gifted defensive back who is remembered in Notre Dame lore for a spectacular open-field, touchdown-saving tackle of Army fullback Doc Blanchard, a play that preserved a 0-0 tie and the Irish's unbeaten 1946 record.

The son of a Connellsville, Pa., railroad worker had a special knack for calling the right plays, getting the ball in the right hands and crossing up defenses. Lujack was an accurate thrower who moved gracefully and reacted instinctively under pressure. The two-time consensus All-American refined his skills by working with Chicago Bears quarterback Sid Luckman, football's premier T-formation quarterback.

Lujack, who had finished third in the 1946 Heisman voting, guided the Fighting Irish through a 1947 season in which they never trailed any opponent. The Irish posted three consecutive shutouts and only Northwestern scored more than one touchdown. The offense, with Lujack throwing for 777 yards and nine touchdowns, averaged 32.3 points.

Lujack went on to play four seasons with the Bears, first as Luckman's backup and later as the starter. He led the team in scoring all four years, intercepted eight passes as a rookie and threw for an NFL-record 468 yards in one memorable 1949 game. The two-time Pro Bowler retired to become Notre Dame's backfield coach in 1952, a job he held for two years.

The do-everything Lujack also won praise as an outstanding punter.

Leon Hart (right) receives his Heisman from Wilbur Jurden, president of the Downtown Athletic Club.

LEON HART

He was a human wrecking ball, a hard-charging enforcer who never tasted defeat in four seasons at Notre Dame. Leon Hart also won praise for the pass-catching finesse that frustrated smaller defenders and the non-stop motor that drove one of the Fighting Irish's most revered two-way performers. Big No. 82 was a multi-faceted weapon, a playmaking end for teams that won three national championships and narrowly missed a fourth.

Nobody made a bigger impact for the four Frank Leahy-coached teams that compiled an incredible 36-0-2 record from 1946-49. Hart arrived as a 6-foot-4, 225-pound freshman who was granted immediate eligibility under a special wartime rule. He left as a 245-pound Heisman Trophy and Maxwell Award winner, four-year letterman and two-time consensus All-American.

Off the field, Hart was a physical specimen with classic good looks, an engaging personality and an aptitude for engineering, which showed up in his studies. But charm turned to intensity and social skills gave way to brute force when he put on the golden helmet and began throwing his weight around on game day.

Leahy deployed his weapon in many ways. Hart, bigger than many defensive linemen of his era, could clear running room for backs, carry the ball on end-around plays, line up as a pile-driving fullback in short-yardage situations or use his speed and soft hands as a receiver for such passers as Johnny Lujack, Frank Tripucka and Bob Williams. Defensively, Hart was a force, whether containing and knocking out interference on sweeps or bull-rushing the quarterback.

Hart was especially dangerous after the catch. For years after his Notre Dame departure, fans talked about the short 1948 pass he caught from Tripucka during a 14-14 tie against Southern Cal. Hart rambled 35 yards with the pass, shedding eight Trojan tacklers en route to the goal line. It was one of the more spectacular of his 13 TD passes on 49 career receptions.

Hart and teammate Jim Martin, who played tackle and end, were double-duty ironmen. As a senior, Hart was a force on both sides of the ball, a co-captain who called defensive signals while leading the Irish to a 10-0 record. Opposing coaches learned to avoid the kid from Turtle Creek, Pa.

"He is the chief reason why opposing teams find it almost impossible to pass against Notre Dame this year," wrote Braven Dyer in a 1949 column for the *Los Angeles Times*. "He bulls in from his end position and virtually knocks the blocker, or blockers, right into the passer. There's no defense for Leon Hart."

That 1949 season was special for several reasons. Not only did the Fighting Irish post a perfect record and win their third national title in four years, Hart won the Heisman Trophy—only the second time the prestigious award had gone to a lineman. He was so high on the sports radar screen that the *Associated Press* named him its male athlete of the year.

After his college career, Hart played eight seasons with the NFL's Detroit Lions, contributing to three championship teams. He was an All-Pro and Pro Bowl selection after the 1951 season.

JOHN LATTNER

HEISMAN TROPHY 1953

Speed and power did not rank high on John Lattner's football resume. Neither did strength, agility or a not-ready-for-prime-time body that lulled opponents into a false sense of security. He was an enigma, an esoteric superstar who confounded skeptics en route to lasting fame as one of the greatest players in Notre Dame's storied history.

Lattner's weakness was that he didn't have that one special skill that gave him a Jim Brown or Sammy Baugh-like status. His strength was the incredible versatility that made him a serious threat as a runner, passer, blocker, receiver, return man, punter and tackler—skills he displayed weekly for Fighting Irish coach Frank Leahy as one of Notre Dame's last two-way performers.

"He doesn't look that fast, and isn't," wrote *Detroit Free Press* sports editor Lyall Smith in 1952 after watching the 6-foot-1, 190-pound halfback run for 98 yards, catch two passes for 46 more and return an interception 28 yards to set up a touchdown during a 27-21 upset of Oklahoma. "He violates one of the first precepts handed a good ballcarrier by running upright instead of putting his head down. He looks like a good target for any tackler.

"But Oklahomans, at least, will claim that mirages are not confined to the great Southwest. He is hard to hit, harder to bring down, harder than that to throw for a loss."

Such was Lattner's magic that he did not lead the Fighting Irish in rushing, passing, receiving or scoring as a senior in 1953, a 9-0-1 season that ended with Notre Dame ranked No. 2 in the final *Associated Press* poll behind Maryland. But he still edged Minnesota's Paul Giel for the Heisman Trophy. Lattner also was awarded his second straight Maxwell Award as the country's top collegiate player and a second straight consensus All-America citation.

The Chicago-born star labored on the practice field with the other freshmen in 1950, a frustrating 4-4-1 season for the proud Leahy. "Lattner could make the varsity right now," groused frustrated Notre Dame athletic director Moose Krause midway through the season. "And I don't mean the traveling squad. He could play a lot, an awful lot."

That wasn't a problem from 1951-53, when Lattner did play at lot—40 to 50 minutes a game as a do-everything halfback and instinctive defensive back. The Irish posted consecutive 7-2-1 seasons in 1951 and '52 with Lattner also handling punting and return duties. His career numbers demonstrate the versatility that earned him national respect.

Lattner set a career Notre Dame record for all-purpose yards (rushing, receiving, runbacks) that stood until 1979. After gaining 16.1 yards per punt return in 1952, he averaged 41.4 yards on eight kickoff returns (with two touchdowns) in 1953. He ran for 1,724 yards from scrimmage (an impressive 4.95 yards per carry), caught 39 passes and intercepted 13.

And he finished his career with the same level of national celebrity achieved by Notre Dame predecessor Johnny Lujack. But Lattner, a first-round draft pick by the NFL's Pittsburgh Steelers in 1954, played only one professional season before a serious knee injury ended his football career.

PAUL HORNUNG

His tousled blond hair, matinee-idol looks and fun-loving personality made Paul Hornung a perfect fit for the Golden Dome. His play-making ability as the against-all-odds quarterback for one of the weakest teams in Notre Dame history made him a more controversial fit for the 1956 Heisman Trophy. The Louisville-born "Golden Boy" charmed the college football world with his smile and conquered it with his do-everything skill and versatility.

Hornung spent his final two Notre Dame seasons as a quarterback, the successor to 1954 consensus All-American Ralph Guglielmi. But the 6-foot-2, 205-pounder also played halfback, fullback and safety for the Fighting Irish and he was an outstanding kicker who even earned a basketball letter before giving up the sport to concentrate on football. As a halfback and fullback in his 1954 sophomore season, Hornung averaged 6.9 yards on 23 carries. As a part-time defender, he intercepted 10 passes in three varsity seasons.

"Paul Hornung," said former Fighting Irish coach Frank Leahy before the 1955 season, "will be the greatest quarterback Notre Dame ever had. He runs like a mower going through grass. Tacklers just fall off him. His kicking—why when he reported to me as a freshman, he could punt 80 yards and placekick over the crossbar from 70 yards."

Leahy, the normally praise-challenged coach who recruited Hornung before retiring after the 1953 season, obviously exaggerated his kicking prowess. But it quickly became apparent this was no ordinary athlete. While leading the 1955 Fighting Irish to an 8-2 record and No. 9 ranking in the final Associated Press poll, Hornung piled up 1,215 total yards (743 passing, 472 rushing) while returning six kickoffs for 109 yards, intercepting five passes and scoring 47 points. Mr. Versatility, who engineered a 21-7 upset of No. 4-ranked Navy, finished fifth in the Heisman voting.

If there was any sense that 1956 would be a special

season at Notre Dame, it disappeared quickly under the weight of crippling injuries. The Irish didn't just lose eight games, they were manhandled by such scores as 47-14 (Michigan State), 40-0 (Oklahoma), 33-7 (Navy), 26-13 (Pittsburgh) and 48-8 (Iowa). The one bright spot was Hornung, who staged a one-man show.

He ranked second nationally in total offense with 1,337 yards, accounted for more than half of the Irish points with his arm, feet and leg, returned 16 kickoffs for 496 yards and four punts for 63, and intercepted two passes. His numbers were generated behind an offensive line that was not overly proficient at opening holes or protecting him on pass attempts and his return yardage was a testament to his speed and running instincts.

A month after the season, as

Paul Hornung (left) shares a Heisman moment with coach Terry Brennan.

Hornung was leaving class, he was informed that he had won the Heisman, a shocking revelation. "I can't believe it," he said after narrowly outpointing Tennessee's Johnny Majors and Oklahoma's Tommy McDonald. "I didn't think I was even up for consideration." It marked the only time the prestigious award has gone to a player from a losing team.

The playboy image that became Hornung's trademark surfaced after he joined the NFL's Green Bay Packers. Over nine professional seasons, Hornung won three NFL scoring titles, four championship rings and praise as one of football's most versatile running backs.

JOHN HUARTE

He is the Roy Hobbs of Notre Dame football, a sidearming quarterback who rose from depth-chart obscurity to Heisman glory in one magical season. John Huarte also came within a few minutes of leading Ara Parseghian's 1964 Fighting Irish to a stunning national championship. The mild-mannered Californian was a storybook-worthy apparition, the classic underdog for the ultimate over-achieving team.

Huarte was not even a blip on the Notre Dame radar screen when new coach Parseghian named him starting quarterback, the chosen one to lead the school back to respectability after a five-year, 19-30 skid under coaches Joe Kuharich and Hugh Devore. The 6-foot, 180-pound senior had not even earned a letter. He was injured most of his sophomore season, buried on Devore's depth chart in 1963 as the Fighting Irish finished 2-7.

"I feel fortunate to have won (the Heisman)," Huarte told *The Sporting News* two decades later. "I was an unknown most of that year, and I just had a perfect season. All I ever wanted to do was win some games."

With Huarte throwing touchdown passes of 61 and 42 yards to Jack Snow, Notre Dame upset Wisconsin, 31-7, in a rousing road opener that set a tone for the entire season. Fans got their first look at Parseghian's new-breed Fighting Irish at Notre Dame Stadium the next week and watched them blow away a good Purdue team, 34-15. The pattern continued with wins over Air Force, UCLA, Stanford and Navy that vaulted the Irish to the top of the *Associated Press* poll.

Much of that success could be traced directly to the unlikely Huarte-Snow combination, which had clicked on 43 passes for 776 yards and seven TDs through seven games. Snow also was a Parseghian "hunch," a former defensive end and wingback who

John Huarte had an unmistakable Heisman look in '64.

rose to consensus All-American status in his 60-catch, nine-touchdown senior season.

The Irish, ranked No. 1 in both wire-service polls, were 9-0 as they entered their season-ending game against USC at the Los Angeles Coliseum. Only the Trojans, three-time losers and 12-point underdogs, stood between Notre Dame and its first national championship since 1949—a title that seemed inevitable as the Fighting Irish built a 17-0 halftime lead. But Huarte, who connected on 18-of-29 passes for 272 yards and a 21-yard TD strike to Snow, could not deliver the knockout punch.

USC scored three second-half touchdowns, the back-breaker coming with 1:33 to play, and Notre Dame lost a touchdown on a holding penalty. The Irish also lost the game, and the championship, 20-17. Not lost, however, was the Heisman recognition, accorded four days before the USC game, for Huarte—perhaps the biggest longshot winner in the award's long history.

When the dust had cleared, Huarte owned 12 Notre Dame records and numerous other national accolades, including consensus All-American status. He finished third nationally in total offense (2,069 yards), set an Irish single-season record for passing yards (2,062) and tied the Notre Dame mark for touchdown passes (16).

The well-timed breakthrough performance also gained Huarte a rich contract from the AFL's New York Jets, who outbid the NFL's Philadelphia Eagles for his services. But Huarte's magic ran out in the professional ranks. He was seldom more than a backup over a six-year AFL/NFL career that included stints with Boston, Philadelphia, Kansas City and Chicago. He also played in the World Football League.

TIM BROWN

He was instant mayhem, a life-sapping weapon at the creative disposal of Notre Dame coach Lou Holtz. When Tim Brown got his hands on the ball, good things usually happened for the guys in blue and gold. So Holtz made sure that he did—he handed, passed and pitched it to him while also utilizing Brown as an electrifying kick- and punt-return specialist.

The speedy 6-foot, 192-pound Dallas-born flanker was a bona fide playmaker. He had lightning quickness, the ability to freeze defenders with subtle feints and dazzling cuts against the grain. He had soft, sure hands and was tough enough to operate in traffic. He was versatile, instinctive and intelligent. And the hint of cockiness that gave Brown his athletic edge was balanced by a modest, unassuming personality and strong religious background.

"We'll hand it to him, we'll throw it to him and we'll let them kick it to him," said Holtz, who lined up his young star as a wideout, wingback and tailback in the full-house backfield formations he employed in 1986 and '87. "You can never minimize the effect a Tim Brown has on a football team or a football game."

For his first two Notre Dame seasons, Brown had only a minimal effect. He fumbled the opening kick-off in the first game of his freshman year against Purdue and was something of an afterthought in coach Gerry Faust's run-oriented offense in 1984 and '85. But when Holtz was handed the Irish coaching reins in 1986, he took one look at Brown and began dreaming up ways to get him the ball.

After averaging 26.5 receptions and 13.9 yards per catch under Faust, Brown emerged as one of the college game's most dangerous threats as the Irish struggled to a 5-6 record in 1986. He averaged 20.2 yards on 45 catches, rushed for 254 yards on 59 carries and turned heads with his big-play ability. Brown returned a kickoff 96 yards for a touchdown against LSU and another 95 yards against Air Force; he caught TD passes of 84 yards against SMU and 77 against Navy and his 56-yard punt return set up a late field goal in a memorable comeback win over Southern Cal.

Brown's 1987 Heisman march gained momentum during a 31-8 win over Michigan State at Notre Dame Stadium. In the first quarter of the September 19 game against the eventual Big Ten Conference champions, he dazzled a packed house by returning a punt 71 yards for a touchdown—and then provided an encore less than 2 minutes later. His second consecutive TD punt return, this one a 66-yarder, vaulted him to national prominence.

Brown, with opponents understandably kicking away from him the rest of the season, went on to pile up 1,847 all-purpose yards (sixth nationally at 167.9 yards per game) as a senior while averaging 14.2 per play and 21.7 on 39 receptions. Those flashy numbers helped the Irish post an 8-3 regular-season record en route to a Cotton Bowl berth and earned Brown distinction as Notre Dame's seventh Heisman Trophy winner—a receiver on a list traditionally dominated by quarterbacks and running backs.

Brown, who is second on Notre Dame's career list for pass reception yards (2,493), has risen to an even higher plateau as a professional. The Los Angeles Raiders' first-round (sixth overall) 1988 draft pick is a Pro Bowl regular and a member of the NFL's exclusive 1,000-catch club. He ranks third all-time in receptions.

The first great ballcarrier in Notre Dame history also was a touchdown-scoring machine, big-play defender, punter and fearless competitor for teams that posted a four-year mark of 28-6-4. The 5-10, 175-pound fullback was extraordinary in 1903, scoring 105 points (11.7 per game) for an 8-0-1 team that outpointed opponents, 291-0. Salmon, a two-time captain and Notre Dame coach in 1904, scored 36 career TDs, still third-most in school history.

HARRY "RED" MILLER
1906-09

The first of five football-playing brothers at Notre Dame earned All-American consideration as a senior in 1909. The 6-foot Ohioan, older brother of Four Horseman star Don Miller and father of 1943 consensus All-American Creighton Miller, was an offensive and defensive halfback fixture for four seasons and one of the school's first outstanding players. Notre Dame compiled a 27-2-2 record in Miller's four seasons.

GUS DORAIS
1910-13

Notre Dame's first consensus All-American is credited with popularizing the forward pass in a historic 1913 performance against Army. The 5-7 Dorais, a quarterback and ballhawking defender, threw for 243 yards—40 on a TD pass to Knute Rockne—in a 35-13 rout that vaulted Notre Dame into national prominence. Dorais, who gained later distinction as a college and professional coach, led the Fighting Irish to three straight undefeated seasons while experiencing only one loss.

RAY EICHENLAUB
1911-14

The 6-foot, 210-pound Eichenlaub was the battering-ram fullback who made life easier for pioneering passer Gus Dorais. A four-year starter who scored 176 career points, Eichenlaub also was a fine blocker and receiver for teams that posted three unbeaten seasons and a 26-2-2 record. The big Ohioan scored 12 TDs in 1913, two in the 35-13 win at Army that gave the Notre Dame program national stature.

FRANK RYDZEWSKI 1915-17

At 6-1 and 214 pounds, Rydzewski was a two-way center in the final three seasons of Jesse Harper's coaching reign. Rydzewski, a two-year starter who became Notre Dame's second consensus All-American as a senior, helped the Fighting Irish compile a 21-3-1 three-year record. He later played seven seasons in a professional career that included stints for both teams in his native Chicago.

GEORGE GIPP ▶
1917-20

The Gipp legend was spawned by the exploits of the most athletically gifted player in Notre Dame's first half century. The 6-foot Michigan phenom led coach Knute Rockne's first three teams in rushing, passing and scoring while also excelling as a defensive back and kicker. Gipp, the school's career rushing leader for almost six decades, led the Irish to a four-year record of 27-2-3 while garnering consensus All-American honors in 1920, a few weeks before he died of pneumonia.

EDDIE ANDERSON 1918-21

The 5-10, 164-pound Iowan, a three-year teammate of George Gipp, was an undersized two-way end in the first four seasons of Knute Rockne's coaching tenure. The four-year starter and two-time Notre Dame receiving leader played for teams that posted a 28-1 record from 1919-21, earning consensus All-American honors as a senior. Anderson gained post-Irish distinction as a doctor and successful coach who posted 201 wins, 129 in 21 seasons at Holy Cross.

HEARTLEY ANDERSON
1918-21

The 5-11, 170-pound "Hunk" followed Michigan childhood friend George Gipp to Notre Dame and became one of his top blockers. Anderson was a starting two-way guard for Knute Rockne's first four teams, an All-American in 1921 when the Fighting Irish finished 10-1. He later served as Rockne's assistant and then carved out a 16-9-2 head coaching record in the three seasons (1931-33) following Rockne's death.

PAUL CASTNER
1920-22

A gifted fullback and kick returner who earned All-American consideration as a junior and senior, the 190-pound Castner is best remembered for a season-ending 1922 injury that opened the door for an all-Four Horsemen backfield. Castner, who scored all 27 points (3 TDs, 2 field goals, 3 extra-point kicks) in a 1922 win over Indiana, still holds Notre Dame kickoff-return records for career average (36.5) and single-game yardage (253). He also excelled in baseball and pitched six games for the 1923 Chicago White Sox.

JIM CROWLEY
1922-24

The 5-11 halfback, one of the celebrated Four Horsemen, rushed for 1,841 yards and 15 TDs over a 27-2-1 three-year span that produced Knute Rockne's first championship (1924). "Sleepy Jim," the drowsy-eyed protege of fellow Green Bay native and former Irish player Curly Lambeau, was a quick and shifty runner who piled up 739 yards in his consensus All-American senior season. Crowley later won attention in pro and college football, most notably as coach at Fordham.

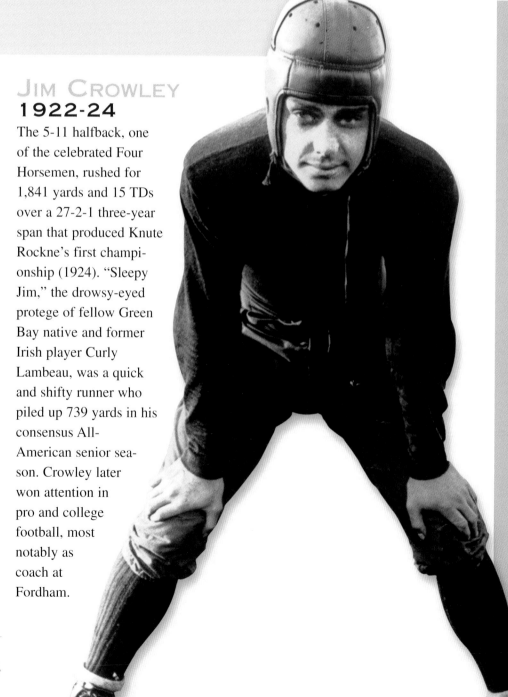

ELMER LAYDEN
1922-24

The fastest of the Four Horsemen thrived as a 162-pound fullback in Knute Rockne's speed-oriented backfield. Layden also was the team's punter and best defender, a ball-hawk who returned two interceptions for TDs and also scored on a three-yard run in a championship-clinching win over Stanford in the 1925 Rose Bowl. Layden, who rushed for 1,296 career yards, later compiled a 47-13-3 record (1934-40) as Notre Dame coach and served as commissioner of the NFL.

HARRY STUHLDREHER 1922-24

He was the brash, fast-thinking quarterback who directed traffic for the 10-0 Irish in their 1924 championship season. Stuhldreher, the smallest of the Four Horsemen at 5-7, completed 25-of-33 passes for 471 yards and four TDs, scored three times on runs and led the team in punt returns in his consensus All-American senior season. The two-year starter from Massillon, Ohio, later won 110 games as a coach at Villanova and Wisconsin.

DON MILLER 1922-24

Knute Rockne proclaimed the 5-11 Miller "the greatest open-field runner I ever had." An All-American in 1923, he was the only member of the Four Horsemen who did not earn that status in Notre Dame's 1924 championship season—even though he led the team with 763 rushing yards and 16 receptions. The shifty and always-dangerous Miller ran for 1,933 career yards and still ranks second all-time with 6.8 yards per carry.

ADAM WALSH 1922-24

The 187-pound Walsh, a three-sport star, was the center and inspirational leader of the "Seven Mules" line that cleared paths for the Four Horsemen. He also was captain of the undefeated 1924 team that ranks among the greatest in history. In a 13-7 win over Army that season, Walsh played with two broken hands but never missed a snap, led the team in tackles and even intercepted a pass that secured victory.

JOE BOLAND 1924-26

The 221-pound Boland was a good two-way tackle under Knute Rockne, but his greatest contributions to Notre Dame football came in later years as a nationally recognized football broadcaster for CBS and WSBT-Radio in South Bend. Boland was a blocker for the Four Horsemen in 1924, a line coach under Elmer Layden from 1934-40 and a local personality and "Voice of the Irish" until his death in 1960.

ART BOERINGER ▶
1925-26

From second-string center in 1925 to consensus All-American a year later, "Bud" Boeringer made a quantum leap into the Notre Dame spotlight. In the process, the rugged 6-1, 176-pound two-way lineman helped anchor a 1926 team that finished 9-1 and missed an undefeated season only because of a stunning 19-0 loss to Carnegie Tech in the second-to-last game of the season.

CHRISTY FLANAGAN 1925-27

Dubbed the "Lone Horseman" by Grantland Rice, Flanagan carried the banner of the Four Horsemen as Notre Dame's leading rusher in the three seasons following their graduation. The quick and shifty 170-pound Texan, who starred for teams that posted a 23-4-2 record, was at his best in 1927 when he ran for 731 yards and earned All-American honors. The colorful Flanagan finished his career with 1,822 yards and 15 TDs.

JOHN SMITH
1925-27

At 5-9 and 165 pounds, the little man nicknamed "Clipper" manned the trenches as a two-way guard for Knute Rockne-coached teams. What he lacked in size he made up for with quickness and intelligence that translated into consensus All-American honors in 1927, when he served as captain for a 7-1-1 team. The Fighting Irish posted a 23-4-2 record in Smith's three seasons, two of which he operated as a starter.

JACK CHEVIGNY
1926-28

The 5-9 halfback will always be remembered as the man who scored the game-tying third-quarter touchdown in the legendary "Gipper" game of 1928. Chevigny, inspired by coach Knute Rockne's "Win One for the Gipper" speech at halftime of a game against Army, scored on a one-yard run in a contest eventually won by the underdog Fighting Irish, 12-6. Chevigny led the team with 539 rushing yards as a senior.

JACK CANNON
1927-29

The free-spirited 193-pound Ohio native, maybe the best two-way guard in Notre Dame history, was one of the last Irish players to compete without a helmet.

Cannon was a quick, rugged blocker and tackler who helped anchor an undefeated 1929 team that won the first of consecutive Notre Dame national championships. Cannon threw the block that freed Jack Elder on a 96-yard interception return in the 7-0 title-clinching win over Army.

TOM CONLEY 1928-30

The 5-11 Conley was the starting two-way end for Knute Rockne's last two teams—the championship squads of 1929 and '30. Conley, a deep-threat receiver and hard-nosed defender, also was captain of a 1930 team that outscored opponents, 265-74. Overshadowed by such big-play teammates as Frank Carideo, Marchy Schwartz and Marty Brill, Conley earned second-team All-American honors as a senior.

Conley (left) with Rockne

FRANK CARIDEO
1928-30

Notre Dame's first two-time consensus All-American engineered the school's first back-to-back national championships—9-0 and 10-0 masterpieces in 1929 and '30. Though undersized at 5-7 and 172 pounds, Carideo was a heady and instinctive signal-caller who also impacted games as a defensive back, punter and kick returner. The confident New Yorker never led the Irish in rushing or passing, but few quarterbacks have matched his leadership and play-calling skills.

JOHNNY O'BRIEN
1928-30

Never more than a third-string end for teams that posted a 24-4 record and won two national championships, O'Brien is remembered for one special play. Making his only appearance in Notre Dame's 12-6 victory over Army in 1928, O'Brien caught a 32-yard fourth-quarter TD pass from John Niemiec that provided the deciding points in the legendary "Win One for the Gipper" contest at New York's Yankee Stadium.

MARCHY SCHWARTZ 1929-31

A perfect complement to Frank Carideo, Schwartz was a big-play halfback for Irish teams that won consecutive national titles (1929-30) and compiled a 25-2-1 three-year record. The speedy 167-pounder led his team in rushing, passing and scoring as a junior and senior while earning back-to-back consensus All-American citations. Schwartz, a 927-yard rusher in 1930, finished his career with 1,945, second only to George Gipp at the time.

TOMMY YARR 1929-31

The Dabob, Wash., native was another of Knute Rockne's undersized linemen (5-11, 195) who relied on quickness and technique. Yarr was a backup center on Notre Dame's 1929 undefeated championship team, a starter in 1930 when the Irish garnered another title with a 10-0 record. Yarr was an offensive and defensive force in 1931 when he won consensus All-American honors for a team that finished 6-2-1 in the wake of Rockne's tragic death.

JOE KURTH
1930-32

The talented two-way tackle bridged the gap between the Rockne era and a less-prosperous period under coach Hunk Anderson. The 6-2, 197-pound tough guy from Madison, Wis., was a sophomore starter on Rockne's last team, a quick and reliable blocker and tackler for the 10-0 national champs of 1930. He also was a force in 1931 and '32 under Anderson, winning consensus All-American honors as a senior for the 7-2 Irish.

MOOSE KRAUSE
1931-33

Krause is best remembered for the 32 years he spent as Notre Dame's athletic director, but before that he was a second-team All-American lineman, an All-American basketball center, an assistant football coach and head basketball coach for the Irish. The 6-3, 220-pound Chicagoan was an immovable force at tackle, a two-year starter who was recruited by Knute Rockne but played his three varsity seasons under Hunk Anderson.

JACK ROBINSON
1932, '34

Robinson overcame multiple eye operations and the death of his father to become a consensus All-American in 1934. A starting center and defensive lineman in 1932, the 6-3, 200-pounder had a cyst removed from his eye the following May and ended up missing the 1933 season. When finally able to return in 1934, shortly after his father died, Robinson excelled for a team that finished 6-3 in Elmer Layden's first season as coach.

BILL SHAKESPEARE 1933-35

"The Bard" was a do-everything halfback and punter who bridged the gap between coaches Hunk Anderson and Elmer Layden. The 5-11 New Yorker twice led the Fighting Irish in passing, once in rushing and scoring while posting a 40.7-yard career average as a punter. He is best remembered for his game-deciding TD pass to Wayne Millner in Notre Dame's shocking 18-13 win at Ohio State in 1935, a year in which Shakespeare won All-American honors.

WAYNE MILLNER 1933-35

As a 1933 sophomore, Millner blocked an Army punt and recovered it in the end zone for the decisive touchdown in a 13-12 Irish victory. In the 1935 "Game of the Century" against Ohio State, he caught the TD pass that sealed an 18-13 victory. The 6-foot Millner, a three-year ironman end who earned consensus All-American status as a senior, went on to gain Pro Football Hall of Fame distinction for the NFL's Redskins.

ANDY PILNEY 1933-35

Never a starter, the 5-11 Pilney was a three-season contributor at halfback and a hero in the 1935 upset of Ohio State. He set up a fourth-quarter touchdown against the Buckeyes with a 47-yard punt return and 11-yard pass, threw a TD pass to Mike Layden and scrambled 30 yards before being injured to set up the game-winner—a 19-yard completion from Bill Shakespeare to Wayne Millner.

JIM McKENNA 1935

He was the unlikely messenger who delivered the game-deciding play to the huddle in the waning moments of the 1935 "Game of the Century" at Ohio State—a role that shocked and immortalized the reserve quarterback from St. Paul, Minn. McKenna, who wasn't even on the Notre Dame traveling squad, sneaked onto the Columbus-bound train and suited up only because coach Elmer Layden admired his spunk and determination.

CHUCK SWEENEY 1935-37 ▶

When the 6-foot, 179-pound Sweeney ventured from Bloomington, Ill., to South Bend in 1934, he was torn between basketball and football. He played both for two years, finally committing to the sport that earned him consensus All-American status as a senior. Sweeney was an impact two-way end who helped Elmer Layden's Fighting Irish carve out a three-year record of 19-5-3.

ED BEINOR 1936-38

The 6-2, 207-pound "Beefy" was an enforcer for Elmer Layden-coached teams that compiled a 20-5-2 record. A two-year starter at offensive and defensive tackle, Beinor gained national stature as a go-to blocker and fearless run-stopper in 1937 and consensus All-American recognition a year later when a final-game loss to USC cost Notre Dame an unbeaten record and national championship. Beinor also was a world-class shot-putter.

BOB DOVE 1940-42

He was a two-time consensus All-American who bridged the Elmer Layden-Frank Leahy coaching eras. The 6-2, 188-pound Dove was tough and aggressive, a two-way end who could make important receptions, throw key blocks or disrupt offenses with instinctive quickness. He capped a dominant senior season by winning the Knute Rockne Trophy (honoring the nation's top college lineman) before moving on to a nine-year professional career.

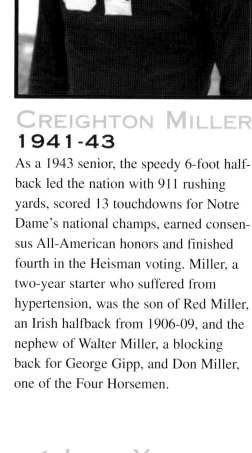

CREIGHTON MILLER
1941-43

As a 1943 senior, the speedy 6-foot half-back led the nation with 911 rushing yards, scored 13 touchdowns for Notre Dame's national champs, earned consensus All-American honors and finished fourth in the Heisman voting. Miller, a two-year starter who suffered from hypertension, was the son of Red Miller, an Irish halfback from 1906-09, and the nephew of Walter Miller, a blocking back for George Gipp, and Don Miller, one of the Four Horsemen.

PAT FILLEY 1941-44

Teammates called him "Peanut," a nickname that only inspired the 5-8, 178-pound Filley to outfight and outsmart bigger opponents as a two-way guard under Frank Leahy. Filley, a junior captain for Leahy's 1943 national champs, was the emotional leader and one of five consensus All-Americans from that team. In 1944 under interim coach Ed McKeever, the South Bend native became Notre Dame's first two-time captain in 25 years.

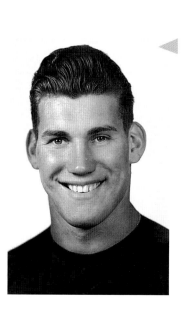

◄ JOHN YONAKOR
1942-43

He was the biggest starter (6-4, 222) on Notre Dame's 1943 championship team and the leading receiver (15 catches, 323 yards). Yonakor, a third-string end in his 1942 junior season, also was a big-play defender who emerged as one of the team's five consensus All-Americans. Yonakor, who doubled as a world-class shot-putter, caught a 30-yard TD pass in a critical 1943 victory over Army.

JIM WHITE
1942-43

At 6-2 and 210 pounds, the big tackle was a force for Notre Dame's offensive and defensive lines in the World War II era. White also was a consensus All-American blocker for a 1943 Fighting Irish championship team that featured backs Angelo Bertelli, Johnny Lujack and Creighton Miller. White was so impressive as a senior that he received votes for the Heisman Trophy—an unusual honor for an interior lineman.

ZYGMONT CZAROBSKI 1942-43, 1946-47

The fun-loving 213-pound strongman from Chicago provided both comic relief and muscle in the trenches for three Frank Leahy-coached championship teams. "Ziggy" was the starting right tackle for the 1943, '46 and '47 champs, his college career interrupted by two years of service in World War II. The 1947 All-American also was a Leahy favorite and one of the most popular players in Notre Dame history.

Coach Brennan and tackle Bronko Nagurski Jr. in 1956

TERRY BRENNAN 1945-48

The 6-foot Milwaukee halfback was an overshadowed but key contributor for three straight undefeated Frank Leahy-coached teams and two national champions. Brennan, a shifty runner and reliable receiver, rushed for 1,249 career yards and led Notre Dame in receptions and scoring as a sophomore and junior. Brennan, who also excelled as a pole vaulter and boxer, followed Leahy as coach in 1954 and compiled a five-year record of 32-18.

GEORGE CONNOR 1946-47

Connor, a post-World War II transfer from Holy Cross, crammed a lot into his two Notre Dame seasons. He was a two-time consensus All-American, won the first Outland Trophy in 1946 and played for two unbeaten championship teams. At 6-3, 225 pounds, he was an offensive and defensive force—one of the all-time greats at his position. Connor later earned Pro Football Hall of Fame induction after starring for his hometown Chicago Bears.

BILL FISCHER 1946-48

The man they called "Moose" was one of the most decorated players in Notre Dame history—a consensus All-American in 1947 and '48, the Outland Trophy winner in '48. The 6-2, 226-pound Chicago-born guard also was an offensive and defensive anchor for teams that finished 8-0-1, 9-0 and 9-0-1 while winning two championships. Fischer, a two-year linemate of powerful George Connor, averaged more than 33 minutes per game in an ironman senior campaign.

JIM MARTIN 1946-49

The former Marine war hero was a four-year starter for Notre Dame teams that compiled a 36-0-2 record and won three national titles. The cat-quick 204-pounder excelled as a two-way end for three years and a defensive end/offensive tackle in 1949 when the Irish switched to a T-formation. The durable Martin, who averaged 40.5 minutes as a senior All-American, went on to play 14 professional seasons.

EMIL SITKO 1946-49

Sitko, a 5-8 bundle of muscle and desire, was a four-year backfield starter and member of three Notre Dame title teams. The Fighting Irish never lost (36-0-2) with Sitko, who led the team in rushing in each of his four seasons while posting 2,226 career yards (second at the time to George Gipp) and 26 touchdowns. Sitko, a 1948 and '49 consensus All-American, won the 1949 Walter Camp Trophy as college football's outstanding player.

BOB WILLIAMS 1948-50

The savvy and resourceful junior quarterback led the 1949 Fighting Irish to a 10-0 record and national championship while earning consensus All-American honors and Heisman Trophy consideration. The 6-1, 180-pounder from Baltimore threw for 1,374 yards and 16 TDs that season, both school records, and followed with a 1,035-yard, 10-touchdown showing as a senior All-American. Williams, known for his passing accuracy, also was a reliable punter.

Williams (9) holds for kicker Vince Meschievitz.

JERRY GROOM
1948-50

In 1948, the 6-3, 210-pound Groom was a backup center for the unbeaten Fighting Irish. In 1949, he started at middle linebacker for the unbeaten national champs. In 1950, the proud Iowan played both positions, clocking 465 minutes in an ironman effort for a team that slid to 4-4-1.

That averaged out at 51.7 minutes per game, a performance that earned the strong, fast and hard-hitting senior and captain consensus All-American honors.

JIM MUTSCHELLER
1949-51

A backup end and defensive back on the 1949 championship team that featured Heisman Trophy-winning end Leon Hart, Mutscheller became Notre Dame's go-to receiver in 1950. He set school single-season records with 35 catches for 426 yards and seven touchdowns as a junior while also leading the team in scoring. The 6-1, 198-pounder from Beaver Falls, Pa., caught 20 more passes in 1951 as a senior captain for a 7-2-1 team.

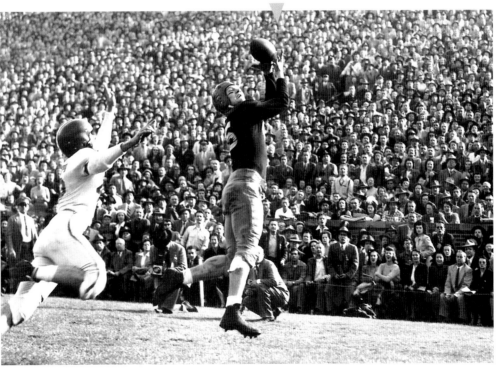

ART HUNTER 1951-53

He was Mr. Versatility for Notre Dame coach Frank Leahy—a starting center in 1951, a two-way end in 1952 (16 catches, 246 yards, 1 TD) and a consensus All-American two-way tackle as a 1953 senior. The 6-3, 221-pound strongman from Ohio averaged 42.3 minutes per game for the 9-0-1 Irish in Leahy's final season while recovering three fumbles, one for a touchdown. Hunter went on to play 11 seasons in the NFL.

NEIL WORDEN
1951-53

There was nothing fancy about the undersized, hard-driving fullback from Milwaukee, who provided both inspiration and power to Frank Leahy's final three teams. The 5-11, 185-pound "Bull" pounded out 2,039 tough career yards and scored 29 touchdowns, leading the Irish twice in rushing (1951 and '53) and three times in scoring. Worden's 859 yards and 11 TDs helped the 9-0-1 Irish garner a No. 2 ranking in 1953.

Worden (48) with teammates John Lattner (14), Tom Carey (2) and Joe Heap (42).

RALPH GUGLIELMI
1951-54

Guglielmi passed for 3,117 yards and 18 touchdowns over four seasons and was a three-year starter. He led Notre Dame to 9-0-1 and 9-1 records in Frank Leahy's final season and Terry Brennan's first. The savvy 6-footer also rushed for 200 yards and 12 TDs, made 10 interceptions and recovered a pair of fumbles as an impact two-way star. Guglielmi was a consensus All-American for the No. 4-ranked Irish in 1954.

FRANK VARRICHIONE 1951-54 ▶

A starting tackle for Frank Leahy's final two Notre Dame teams and Terry Brennan's first, Varrichione (second from top, right photo) is best remembered for his stalling tactic in a 14-14 tie against Iowa in 1953. The 210-pounder ignited controversy when he "fainted" with two seconds remaining in the half, a medical timeout that allowed the Irish to score a touchdown. Notre Dame used a similar tactic late in the game to score again and gain the tie.

DICK LYNCH 1955-57

Lynch is best remembered for the three-yard run that gave Notre Dame a 7-0 win over Oklahoma in a 1957 game at Norman and ended the Sooners' record 47-game winning streak. Lynch, who rushed for 287 yards in '57, caught a team-high 13 passes and returned kicks and punts for the 7-3 Irish in his only season as a starter, scored his memorable TD with 3:50 remaining on a pitch from quarterback Bob Williams.

AL ECUYER
1956-58

Ecuyer, a hard-nosed defensive guard, was one of the few bright lights in Notre Dame's 2-8 1956 season. The 5-10, 190-pounder from New Orleans was more than that in 1957—a consensus All-American for a team that rebounded to 7-3 and a No. 10 AP ranking. Ecuyer, who was credited with 18 tackles in a 1957 loss to Iowa, also earned All-American consideration as a senior co-captain in '58.

NICK PIETROSANTE
1956-58

The 6-2, 215-pound workhorse fullback punished defenders in two seasons as a starter. Pietrosante earned All-American recognition as a junior and senior when he led the Irish in rushing (90 carries, 449 yards; 117, 549) and ranked among team leaders in tackles as a part-time defender. The tireless Pietrosante, who also punted, was the decoy ballcarrier on the memorable 1957 Dick Lynch TD run that ended Oklahoma's record win streak.

MONTY STICKLES
1957-59

Big, tough and fast, Stickles terrorized opponents as a surehanded receiver, run-stopping end and reliable kicker. The versatile New Yorker was a junior All-American in 1958 when he led Notre Dame in receptions (20) and scoring (60 points), a consensus All-American a year later when he averaged 21.4 yards on 11 catches for a team that finished only 5-5. The 6-4, 215-pound Stickles caught 42 career passes, scored 12 TDs and made 110 tackles.

Stickles (80) carries on an end-around in a 1959 game against USC.

NICK BUONICONTI 1959-61

The future Pro Football Hall of Fame linebacker spent most of his college career as an undersized defensive guard for weak teams. At 5-11 and 210 pounds, Buoniconti was lost in the Notre Dame shuffle until an injury to Myron Pottios gave him an unexpected opportunity in his sophomore season. In 1960 he emerged as a full-fledged playmaker; in 1961 the senior co-captain earned All-American recognition for a 5-5 team.

DICK ARRINGTON
1963-65

An outstanding wrestler with tremendous upper-body strength, the 5-11, 232-pound Arrington excelled on both sides of the ball for coach Ara Parseghian. Arrington was a key offensive guard for Heisman-winning quarterback John Huarte in 1964; a starter at both offensive guard and defensive tackle in 1965. Those two teams finished 16-3-1 and Arrington's two-way prowess made him a consensus All-American as a senior.

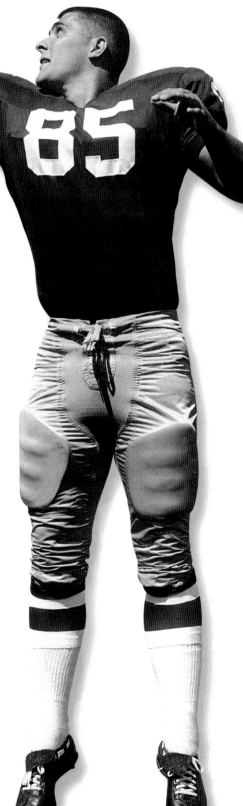

JACK SNOW
1962-64

The 6-2 Californian, a part-time flanker/wingback/ defensive back, exploded into prominence as the go-to senior receiver for Heisman Trophy-winning quarterback John Huarte in 1964. The surehanded Snow posted single-season school records with 60 catches for 1,114 yards and nine TDs as the 9-1 Irish earned a No. 3 national ranking in coach Ara Parseghian's first season. The consensus All-American used that performance as a springboard to an 11-year NFL career.

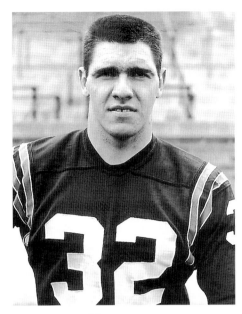

PETE DURANKO
1963-66

At 6-2 and 235 pounds, Duranko gave Ara Parseghian's 1966 national champs a formidable presence on their defensive front wall. The big tackle, granted an extra season of eligibility because of a 1964 injury, made 73 tackles in a final campaign that earned him All-American recognition. Duranko, from Johnstown, Pa., actually began his college career as a fullback and rushed for 93 yards in his 1963 sophomore season.

NICK EDDY
1964-66

The double-threat halfback was the leading rusher and scorer for Notre Dame's 1966 championship team. Eddy, who rushed for a team-leading 582 yards in 1965, totaled 553 on 78 carries as a senior—a whopping average of 7.1. The 195-pound Californian also caught 15 passes, led the team in kickoff returns and scored 10 of his 21 career TDs in a consensus All-American effort that earned him a third-place finish in the Heisman Trophy voting.

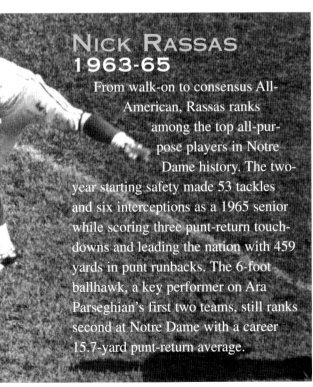

NICK RASSAS
1963-65

From walk-on to consensus All-American, Rassas ranks among the top all-purpose players in Notre Dame history. The two-year starting safety made 53 tackles and six interceptions as a 1965 senior while scoring three punt-return touchdowns and leading the nation with 459 yards in punt runbacks. The 6-foot ballhawk, a key performer on Ara Parseghian's first two teams, still ranks second at Notre Dame with a career 15.7-yard punt-return average.

JIM LYNCH 1964-66

He called signals for a 1965 defense that allowed only 73 points. He was the captain and leading tackler for a 1966 team that allowed 38 points and won a national championship. The 6-1, 225-pound Lynch (No. 61, right) was fast, strong, intense and savvy, the perfect centerpiece for a near-perfect (9-0-1) team. The Ohio-born Lynch also was a consensus All-American and Maxwell Award-winning senior who played 11 seasons in the NFL.

ALAN PAGE 1964-66

The three-year starter at defensive end ranks among the great players in Notre Dame history. A 6-5, 230-pounder with an amazing combination of size, speed and strength, Page (No. 81, below) was one of four consensus All-Americans from the 1966 national champions. The Canton, Ohio, native, earned post-Notre Dame distinction as a Pro Football Hall of Famer and currently is an associate justice on the Minnesota Supreme Court.

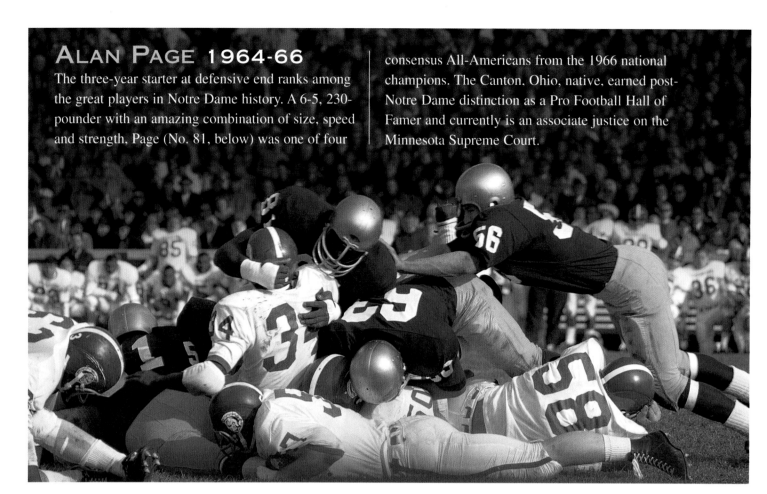

TOM REGNER
1964-66

The 6-1, 245-pound Regner started his career as a defensive tackle and ended it as a consensus All-American offensive guard for the high-scoring 1966 national champs. Everybody marveled at Regner's quick transition when Ara Parseghian moved him from defense to offense in 1965 and the caliber of his play as a senior team leader. Not surprisingly, Regner also was an academic All-American.

JOE AZZARO
1964-67

This Pittsburgh product, the No. 1 kicker for Ara Parseghian's early teams, is best remembered for his role in Notre Dame's epic 1966 showdown against Michigan State. Azzaro connected on a 28-yard fourth-quarter field goal that gave Notre Dame a 10-10 tie in one of the most celebrated—and controversial—battles of all time. But he also missed a 41-yarder with 4:41 remaining that would have given the Irish an outright victory.

KEVIN HARDY 1964-67

He played next to Alan Page as a defensive tackle for the 1966 national champs and Mike McCoy as a defensive end in his 1967 senior season. Hardy, a two-time All-American, was a strong, quick pass-rushing force wherever he played, one of the hardest hitters in Notre Dame history. The 6-5, 270-pound Californian also was a great athlete who lettered in baseball and basketball as well as football.

TOM SCHOEN **1965-67**

Schoen, a speedy quarterback-turned-safety, intercepted seven passes, scored two touchdowns and led the 1966 national champions in punt-return yardage. But it wasn't until his 1967 senior season that he became a consensus All-American. The instinctive 5-11 Ohioan led the 8-2 Fighting Irish with four interceptions and returned 42 punts for 447 yards—a school-record 167 of those coming in a 38-0 win over Pittsburgh.

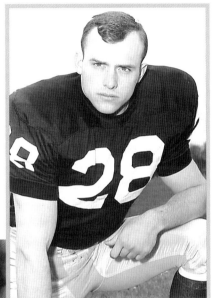

ROCKY BLEIER
1965-67

Best known as the former Vietnam vet who overcame potentially career-ending war injuries to help the Pittsburgh Steelers win four Super Bowls, Bleier first gained recognition as a starting halfback for Notre Dame's undefeated 1966 national champions and captain of its 8-2 team in 1967. The 5-11, 195-pounder ran for 784 yards and 11 touchdowns and caught 36 passes for 422 yards and three TDs in his three-year varsity career.

TERRY HANRATTY 1966-68

He is best remembered as the sophomore quarterback who led Notre Dame to a 1966 national title. But Hanratty actually was a consistent three-year performer whose teams posted a 24-4-2 record. The 6-1 Hanratty, who is inexorably linked to favorite receiver Jim Seymour, completed 304-of-550 career passes for 4,152 yards and 27 touchdowns while running for 586 yards and 16 TDs. He was a consensus All-American as a senior.

COLEY O'BRIEN
1966-68

The 5-11 Virginian was a capable quarterback with unfortunate timing—his three varsity seasons were spent as a backup to Terry Hanratty. But O'Brien will always be remembered for his championship-saving role in 1966. He replaced the injured Hanratty early in the Michigan State game and salvaged a 10-10 tie and then directed a season-ending 51-0 win over USC. O'Brien threw for five career TDs and ran for six others.

BOB GLADIEUX
1966-68

Although remembered primarily for the 34-yard touchdown pass he caught from Coley O'Brien in Notre Dame's 10-10 tie with Michigan State in 1966, Gladieux actually enjoyed a solid three-year career. After two seasons as a backup halfback, the shifty 5-11 senior blossomed for the 7-2-1 Irish of 1968, rushing for 713 yards and 12 touchdowns, catching 37 passes for 442 yards and two TDs and returning six punts and 11 kickoffs.

GEORGE KUNZ
1966-68

A tight end and defensive tackle who saw brief duty in an injury-marred sophomore season for the 1966 national champs, Kunz evolved into a dominant consensus All-American offensive tackle and an 11-year lineman in the NFL. Few players could match the mobility and outstanding technique of the 6-5, 228-pound Californian, who was a key blocker for teams that posted a two-year record of 15-4-1 and averaged 35.7 points per game.

JIM SEYMOUR 1966-68

"Hanratty-to-Seymour" was the battle cry for seasons that produced a 24-4-2 record and one national title. The 6-4, 205-pound Seymour was a go-to pass-catcher with excellent size, speed and hands. He led Notre Dame in receiving all three of his varsity seasons and his 2,113 career yards and 16 TD catches still rank high on the school charts. The three-time All-American holds single-game records for catches (13) and yards (276).

MIKE McCOY 1967-69

He was a 6-5, 270-pound defensive monster who could overpower blockers or zip past them with surprising quickness. McCoy was so dominant in his consensus All-American senior season that he finished sixth in the Heisman voting—unusual respect for a lineman. A two-year starter for teams that posted a 15-4-2 record, the Erie, Pa., native went on to play 10 seasons in the NFL.

LARRY DINARDO
1968-70

The first of two brothers who were consensus All-American offensive guards at Notre Dame, the 6-1, 243-pound DiNardo was a three-year starter and a key operative during the high-powered Joe Theismann years. As a senior co-captain, the technique-perfect New Yorker blocked for a team that averaged a school-record 510.5 yards per game en route to a 10-1 record and No. 2 AP ranking. DiNardo also was an academic All-American.

JOE THEISMANN
1968-70

Few quarterbacks can match Theismann's two-year, 18-3-1 run as a starter at Notre Dame. The strong-armed and savvy 6-footer was prolific as a senior All-American when he passed for 2,529 yards and 16 touchdowns and ran for 406 yards and six TDs. The offense that season averaged a whopping 510.5 yards and 30 points per game and Theismann ran for two TDs and passed for another in a Cotton Bowl win over Texas.

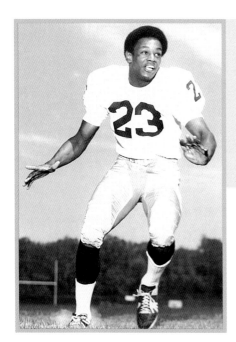

CLARENCE ELLIS 1969-71

The quick, athletic Ellis, leader of the Fighting Irish secondary for three seasons, was a two-time All-American cornerback (consensus in 1971) who played in only five losing games. Seven of his 13 career interceptions came in 1970, when the Irish posted a 10-1 record, and three more came in an 8-2 senior campaign. The ballhawking 6-footer earned defensive MVP honors in Notre Dame's 24-11 win over Texas in the 1971 Cotton Bowl.

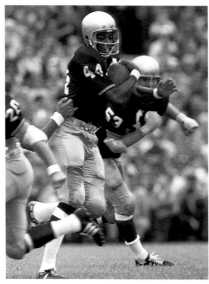

TOM GATEWOOD
1969-71

The fast, silky-smooth receiver from Baltimore, Joe Theismann's favorite target for two seasons, still holds numerous pass-catching records at Notre Dame. The two-time All-American (consensus as a 1970 junior) led Irish receivers in each of his three varsity seasons and finished with 157 catches for 2,283 yards and 19 TDs. Gatewood, who had 77 receptions for the 10-1 Irish in 1970, was a senior co-captain for an 8-2 team in 1971.

WALT PATULSKI
1969-71

He started every game for three years at left defensive end and was co-captain for an 8-2 team in his consensus All-American senior campaign. At 6-6 and 235 pounds, the talented New Yorker overpowered opponents who were always surprised by his speed and mobility. Patulski was so dominant in 1971 that he received Heisman votes, won the Lombardi Award (outstanding college lineman) and was named UPI's Lineman of the Year.

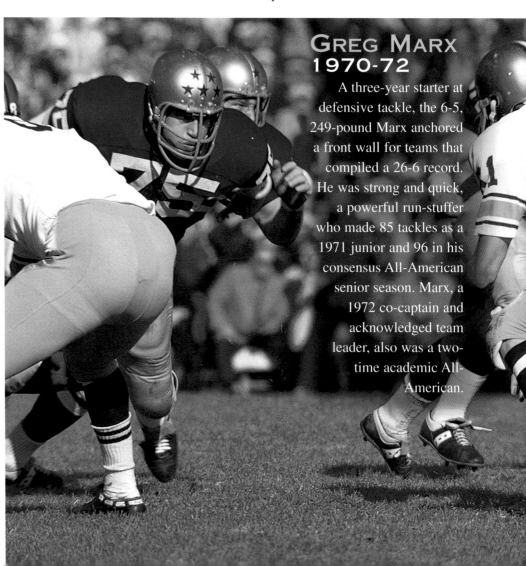

GREG MARX
1970-72

A three-year starter at defensive tackle, the 6-5, 249-pound Marx anchored a front wall for teams that compiled a 26-6 record. He was strong and quick, a powerful run-stuffer who made 85 tackles as a 1971 junior and 96 in his consensus All-American senior season. Marx, a 1972 co-captain and acknowledged team leader, also was a two-time academic All-American.

DAVE CASPER 1971-73

Before his 11-year Pro Football Hall of Fame career, the 6-3, 243-pound Casper saw action at Notre Dame as an offensive tackle, wide receiver and finally, in a consensus All-American senior season, tight end. He was a tri-captain on the 1973 team that finished 11-0 and clinched a national championship with a 24-23 Sugar Bowl win over Alabama. Casper's 30-yard catch in that classic set up Bob Thomas' deciding field goal.

MIKE TOWNSEND
1971-73

The athletic cornerback jumped into the Notre Dame spotlight in his junior season by intercepting a nation-leading 10 passes—a still-standing school record. As a senior tri-captain and free safety in 1973, Townsend backstopped a defense that allowed only 89 points en route to an 11-0 record and national championship. The 6-3 Ohioan picked off three more passes and recovered three fumbles in his consensus All-American final campaign.

TOM CLEMENTS 1972-74

The quarterback for Ara Parseghian's final three teams was nothing if not consistent. He threw for 1,163 yards as a sophomore, 882 as a junior and 1,549 as a senior with eight TD passes each year. His teams finished 8-3, 11-0 and 10-2 and Clements directed the 1973 Irish to a national title that was sealed by his MVP effort in the Sugar Bowl. The 1974 All-American later excelled in the CFL, earning election to the Canadian Football Hall of Fame.

PETE DEMMERLE 1972-74

He was a go-to possession receiver for quarterback Tom Clements and a key figure on the 1973 championship team. The 6-1 end, who also was a good blocker, caught 26 passes in his junior season and made three receptions in Notre Dame's title-clinching 24-23 Sugar Bowl win over Alabama. He also caught a critical two-point conversion pass against the Crimson Tide. Demmerle made 43 receptions for 667 yards and six TDs in his consensus All-American senior campaign.

GERRY DiNARDO
1972-74

The 6-1, 242-pound DiNardo matched the exploits of older brother Larry as a three-year starter at offensive guard and a senior consensus All-American. Gerry, in fact, reached one goal his brother did not—he played for a national championship team in 1973 and helped clear paths for backs who rushed for a school-record 3,502 yards. In DiNardo's senior year, the Fighting Irish finished 10-2.

MIKE FANNING
1972-74

The 6-6, 250-pound Fanning, who doubled as an outstanding college wrestler, was part of a heavyweight defensive line that included Ross Browner, Steve Niehaus and Jim Stock in Notre Dame's 1973 championship season. The quick-footed, pass-rush wizard from Tulsa, Okla., made 85 tackles, including 12 for a minus-52 yards, in an All-American senior season for the 10-2 Fighting Irish.

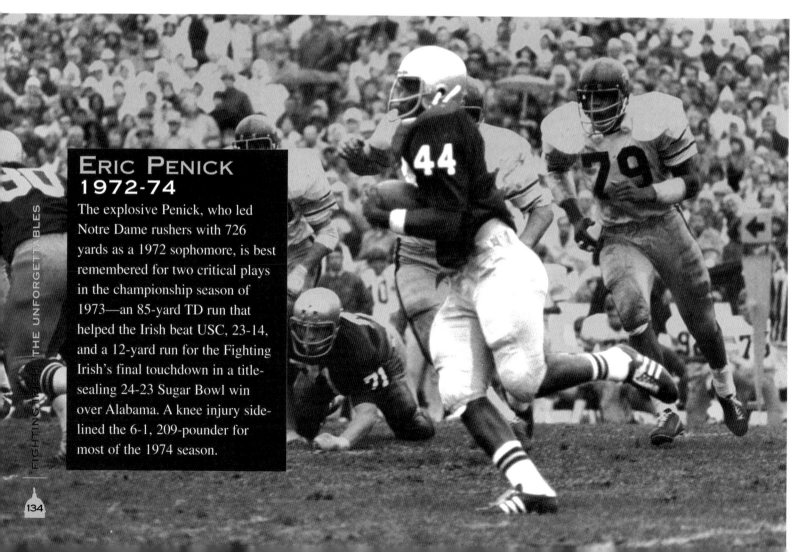

ERIC PENICK
1972-74

The explosive Penick, who led Notre Dame rushers with 726 yards as a 1972 sophomore, is best remembered for two critical plays in the championship season of 1973—an 85-yard TD run that helped the Irish beat USC, 23-14, and a 12-yard run for the Fighting Irish's final touchdown in a title-sealing 24-23 Sugar Bowl win over Alabama. A knee injury sidelined the 6-1, 209-pounder for most of the 1974 season.

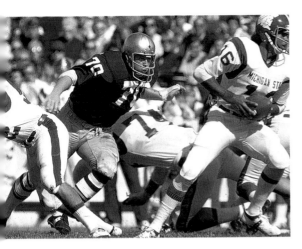

STEVE NIEHAUS 1972-75

Injuries kept the 6-5, 270-pound defensive tackle from being a major factor for the 1973 national champs. But Niehaus made up for lost time in impressive junior and senior seasons. Big, fast and overpowering, the Cincinnati kid anchored the front wall for a 10-2 team in 1974 and made 113 tackles for a 1975 team that finished 8-3 in Dan Devine's first season as coach. He was All-American both seasons, a consensus pick in '75.

ROBIN WEBER 1973-74, 1976

A bit player for three seasons, tight end Weber was immortalized by a 35-yard pass he caught in the waning moments of the 1973 Sugar Bowl—a championship-deciding clash between Notre Dame and Alabama. Weber, who had not caught a regular-season pass, was the surprise target for Tom Clements on a daring third-and-eight play from the Notre Dame 3-yard line that secured a first down and allowed the Irish to run out the clock on a 24-23 victory.

LUTHER BRADLEY
1973, 1975-77

He was a freshman safety for Ara Parseghian's 1973 national title winners and a senior corner-back for Dan Devine's 1977 champions. Along the way the speedy, hard-hitting Bradley picked off a Notre Dame-record 17 passes and became a three-time All-American—a consensus pick in 1977. The 6-2 Bradley, who returned an interception 99 yards for a TD in 1975, sat out the 1974 campaign under suspension.

AL HUNTER 1973, 1975-76

The speedy 6-footer is best remembered for two things—his touchdown on a 93-yard kickoff return that stunned Alabama in the national championship-deciding Sugar Bowl game of 1973 and his legacy as Notre Dame's first 1,000-yard rusher (he ran for 1,058 yards on 233 carries in 1976). Hunter, one of several prominent players who were suspended in 1974, ran for 1,766 career yards and 23 TDs—totals that could have increased if he had stayed for his 1977 senior season.

ROSS BROWNER ▶
1973, 1975-77

The 6-3, 240-pound defensive end was a four-year starter, a two-time consensus All-American, the 1976 Outland Trophy winner, the 1977 Lombardi Trophy winner and a member of two championship teams. He helped Notre Dame post an 11-0 record in 1973 as a freshman and an 11-1 mark in 1977 as a senior. The powerful, often-spectacular playmaker, who missed the 1974 season because of suspension, was one of the great players in Irish history.

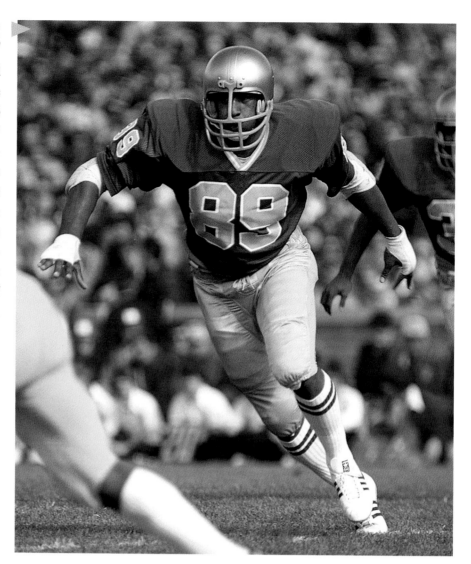

WILLIE FRY
1973, 1975-77

The defensive end tandem of Fry and Ross Browner was unstoppable. Few teams ran outside in their four seasons together and the Irish pass rush was relentless. The Memphis-born Fry was a backup for the 1973 national champs, a key contributor in 1977 when the 11-1 Fighting Irish won another title. Fry, who sat out the 1974 season under suspension, was a co-captain in 1976 and one of four captains in '77.

KEN MACAFEE
1974-77

The most productive tight end in Notre Dame history was a three-time All-American (two-time consensus) and key performer for the 1977 national champs. MacAfee, at 6-5 and 251 pounds, was a nice fit for the position and had instincts and speed to match.

He led the Irish in receiving three straight years and caught 128 passes for 1,759 yards and 15 TDs in his career. MacAfee finished third in the 1977 Heisman voting.

RUDY RUETTIGER 1975

The working-class kid from Joliet, Ill., fulfilled his dream in 1975 when, at age 27, he played for Notre Dame in the final 27 seconds of a game against George Tech. The 5-7 Ruettiger (No. 45, above), an undersized walk-on practice player with contagious enthusiasm, even made a tackle in his cameo and was carried off the field by happy teammates. His story, as told in the 1993 movie *Rudy*, is now the stuff of Notre Dame legend.

JOE MONTANA 1975, 1977-78

The 6-2 Montana, who gained later fame as one of the great quarterbacks in NFL history, was the savvy, ever-cool leader of Notre Dame's 1977 championship team. Known for his dramatic comeback feats, Montana was a two-year starter who showed only flashes of brilliance while posting passing totals of 1,604 yards and 11 touchdowns and 2,010 and 10 TDs. He directed two Cotton Bowl wins—including the dramatic 35-34 comeback against Houston in 1979.

JEROME HEAVENS 1975-78

He was the rugged fullback who broke George Gipp's 58-year-old career rushing record in 1978. The 6-foot, 204-pounder from East St. Louis, Ill., was a three-year starter and two-season Notre Dame rushing leader who piled up 2,682 career yards—994 for the 1977 national champions. Heavens ran for 101 yards in a 38-10 win over Texas in the 1978 Cotton Bowl and 71 in the dramatic 1979 Cotton Bowl comeback win over Houston.

KRIS HAINES 1975-78

A two-year starter who led the Fighting Irish with 32 catches as a senior, Haines is best remembered for his role in Notre Dame's valiant 35-34 comeback win over Houston in the 1979 Cotton Bowl. The 6-foot wideout caught a two-point conversion pass from Joe Montana that cut the one-time 22-point deficit to 6 and then pulled in the tying 8-yard TD pass as the clock expired. A point-after kick capped the stunning rally.

DAVE HUFFMAN 1975-78

The 6-5, 245-pound Texan, the man known for his red elbow pads, was a three-year starter at center and one of the key ingredients of Dan Devine's 1977 championship team. Huffman was an outstanding run and pass blocker who would go on to an 11-year NFL career with the Minnesota Vikings. He was a driving force and leader in '77, a consensus All-American in 1978—teams quarterbacked by Joe Montana.

VAGAS FERGUSON 1976-79

He still holds Notre Dame records for rushing yards in a season (1,437 in 1979) and game (255 against Georgia Tech in 1978) and rushing attempts in a season (301 in 1979). The powerful 6-1 Ferguson was a four-year force, a Cotton Bowl hero for the 1977 national champs and a consensus All-American and tri-captain in 1979. He also was the first Irish player to post consecutive 1,000-yard rushing seasons en route to career totals of 3,472 yards and 32 TDs.

BOB GOLIC 1975-78

One of Notre Dame's greats, the 6-3, 250-pound middle linebacker made 479 career tackles and won distinction as a consensus All-American. Golic, a championship wrestler, was a force for the 1977 national title team, making 146 tackles and three of his six career interceptions. He also earned defensive MVP honors in a Cotton Bowl win over Texas. He made 152 tackles as a 1978 tri-captain before beginning a 14-year NFL career.

JOHN SCULLY 1977-80

The 6-5, 255-pound New Yorker was a freshman backup offensive tackle for the 1977 national champs, a sophomore tackle and backup for star center Dave Huffman. Scully, quick as a cat and fundamentally solid, took over at center for Dan Devine's final two Notre Dame teams, starting all 11 games in 1979 and earning consensus All-American honors as a senior. Scully was a tri-captain for a 1980 team that finished 9-2-1.

BOB CRABLE
1978-81

The 6-3, 225-pound linebacker, a two-time consensus All-American, still holds Notre Dame records for most tackles in a season (187), a game (26) and a career (521). Crable was always a force, whether blocking a last-second field-goal attempt to hold off Michigan in 1979 or recovering a critical 1979 Cotton Bowl fumble against Houston. Crable played at Cincinnati's Moeller High School under Gerry Faust, who became his Notre Dame coach in 1981.

PHIL CARTER
1979-82

He never earned All-American recognition or set records, but the strong and quick 197-pounder from Tacoma, Wash., still ranks fifth on Notre Dame's all-time rushing charts. Carter, a three-year starter at halfback, ran for 822 yards as a sophomore and team-leading totals of 727 and 715 in 1981 and '82. The two-time co-captain under coach Gerry Faust finished his career with 2,409 yards and 14 TDs.

DAVE DUERSON
1979-82

The hard-hitting safety from Muncie, Ind., was an outstanding defender and punt returner for teams coached by Dan Devine and Gerry Faust. The 6-3, 202-pound Duerson was quick and instinctive, a ballhawk who made 12 career interceptions—

seven in his All-American senior season. The 1982 Fighting Irish tri-captain, holder of the school record for punt returns (103), went on to play 11 years in the NFL.

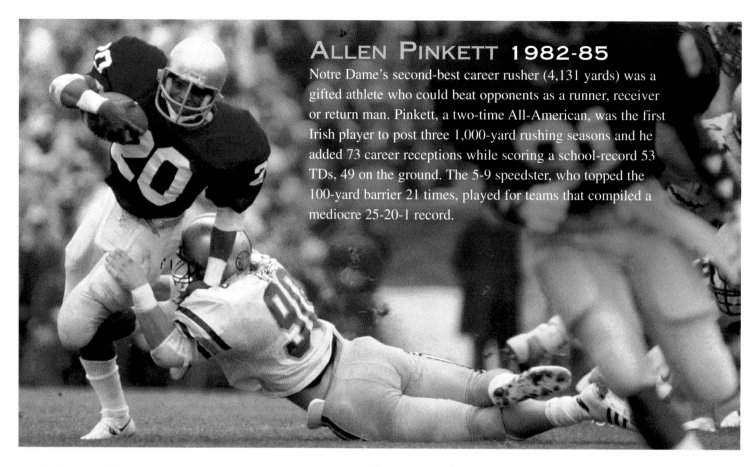

ALLEN PINKETT 1982-85

Notre Dame's second-best career rusher (4,131 yards) was a gifted athlete who could beat opponents as a runner, receiver or return man. Pinkett, a two-time All-American, was the first Irish player to post three 1,000-yard rushing seasons and he added 73 career receptions while scoring a school-record 53 TDs, 49 on the ground. The 5-9 speedster, who topped the 100-yard barrier 21 times, played for teams that compiled a mediocre 25-20-1 record.

STEVE BEUERLEIN 1983-86

The 6-3 Californian, a four-year starter, was one of the best drop-back passers in Notre Dame history. Beuerlein was good enough to supplant senior quarterback Blair Kiel as a freshman and he went on to throw for 6,527 yards and 27 touchdowns. Beuerlein had the good fortune of throwing to Tim Brown and Allen Pinkett, the misfortune of playing for mediocre teams that compiled a 24-22 record. He is still active in the NFL.

JOHN CARNEY 1983-86

Notre Dame's career field-goal leader was a walk-on who went on to score 223 points while posting an extra-point percentage of .933 (70-of-75) and a school-record field-goal percentage of .739 (51-of-69). The strong-legged Floridian, who connected on a school-record 21 field goals in 1986, was extremely accurate inside the 50. He has been one of the NFL's most consistent kickers since 1988.

FRANK STAMS 1984-85, 1987-88

He was a 6-4, 237-pound fullback his first two seasons, a consensus All-American defensive end for the best team in college football as a senior. Stams was a force for Lou Holtz's '88 champs, a bruising hitter who forced two fumbles and covered another in the Irish's critical 31-30 upset of Miami and earned defensive MVP honors in the Fiesta Bowl win over West Virginia. Stams missed the 1986 season because of a broken leg.

MICHAEL STONEBREAKER
1986, 1988, 1990

The 6-1, 228-pound Stonebreaker was a two-time consensus All-American in a career interrupted by academic problems (1987) and injuries (1989). When he did play, the intense and hard-driving linebacker was disruptive. He made 104 tackles and two interceptions for Notre Dame's 1988 national champs, 95 tackles for a 1990 team that finished 9-3. He finished third in Butkus Award voting (the nation's outstanding linebacker) in both 1988 and '90.

PAT TERRELL
1986-89

Terrell is best remembered for his heroics in a 31-30 upset win over Miami that helped secure Notre Dame's 1988 championship. Terrell, a junior wideout-turned-free safety, scored a touchdown on a 60-yard interception return and batted away a last-minute two-point conversion pass by Miami quarterback Steve Walsh that could have won the game. The 6-foot Terrell picked off five passes as a 1989 senior for the 12-1 Irish.

TONY RICE 1987-89

The speedy 6-1, 200-pound playmaker directed 1988 and '89 teams that posted a 24-1 record and won a national championship. A dangerous option quarterback, Rice ran for 700 yards and nine TDs while throwing for 1,176 yards and eight scores as a junior; he ran for 884 yards and passed for 1,122 as a senior All-American. Rice, who scored 23 career TDs, set a school quarterback record with 1,921 rushing yards and his 4,882 total yards rank sixth all time.

RICKY WATTERS
1987-90

The flashy 6-2, 205-pound Watters was a triple-threat weapon for coach Lou Holtz—a flanker and leading receiver for his 1988 national champs, a 1,814-yard career rusher who also returned three punts for TDs. Watters, who would go on to NFL fame as a seven-time 1,000-yard rusher, scored 26 career touchdowns (21 on the ground) for teams that compiled a 41-8 four-year record.

TIM GRUNHARD
1986-89

The powerful Grunhard was a path-clearing guard for Lou Holtz's 1988 national champs and an outstanding long-snapper for the punting unit. The 6-3, 292-pound Chicagoan was a starter for 1988 and '89 teams that compiled a 24-1 record and a second-team All-American as a senior. Grunhard went on to play 11 NFL seasons as a center for the Kansas City Chiefs.

TODD LYGHT
1987-90

He was a 184-pound bundle of energy, a dangerous ballhawk who manned the corner as a three-year starter for the Fighting Irish. Lyght was a sophomore contributor for the 1988 national champs, a consensus All-American in both 1989 and '90 for teams that posted a 21-4 record. He was at his best as a junior when he made 47 tackles and eight of his 11 career interceptions. From 1991-2002, Lyght started 167 of 175 NFL games.

RAGHIB ISMAIL 1988-90

The 5-10, 175-pound "Rocket" was an electrifying performer. A dangerous runner, receiver and return man, the talented flanker topped 1,000 career yards in all three categories and posted 15 touchdowns—six on kick returns, four on receptions and five on runs. Ismail, a two-time All-American (consensus in 1990) and a starter for the 1988 national champs, returned two kickoffs for TDs in the same game twice and averaged a whopping 22 yards per catch.

CHRIS ZORICH 1988-90

The 6-1, 266-pound Chicago strongman was one of the most popular players in Notre Dame history. He also was one of its most decorated—a three-time All-American (two consensus), 1990 Lombardi Trophy winner and recipient of numerous Lineman of the Year citations. Opponents double- and triple-teamed the big nose tackle, who still made 219 tackles. He was a force for the 1988 national champs and teams that posted a 33-4 record.

DEREK BROWN 1988-91

As a freshman, the 6-6, 252-pound prototypical tight end caught two passes for 70 yards in Notre Dame's championship-securing win over West Virginia in the Fiesta Bowl. By the time he finished his senior season, the speedy Floridian ranked as one of the best receiver/blocker tight ends in the country, an All-American who averaged 14.5 yards per catch over his career while scoring eight TDs.

MIRKO JURKOVIC 1988-91

The 6-4, 289-pound Jurkovic was a backup defensive tackle in 1988 when the Fighting Irish won a national title, a starting offensive guard by his junior and senior seasons. The Calumet City, Ill., product was so overpowering and dominant in 1991 that he earned consensus All-American honors for a team that finished 10-3, scored an eye-popping 426 points and beat Florida in the Sugar Bowl.

CRAIG HENTRICH
1989-92

The 6-1 Hentrich is the best all-around kicker in Notre Dame history. For teams that compiled a 41-8-1 record, he averaged a school-record 44.1 yards per punt, connected on 177-of-180 conversions and drilled 39-of-56 field goal attempts while scoring 294 points. Hentrich, who is still a productive NFL punter, was at his best in 1990 when he averaged a Fighting Irish single-season record of 44.9 yards per punt and hit 16-of-20 field goal tries.

RICK MIRER ▶
1989-92

A strong-armed dropback passer, the 6-2, 217-pound Mirer led the Fighting Irish to a 29-7-1 record as a three-year starter. The kid from Goshen, Ind., blossomed as a junior when he passed for 2,117 yards and 18 touchdowns while running for 306 yards and nine TDs. Mirer, who ranks second on Notre Dame's career touchdown pass list with 41, threw 15 as a senior co-captain in 1992 when the fourth-ranked Irish finished 10-1-1.

REGGIE BROOKS 1989-92

After three seasons as a backup running back and cornerback, the 5-8, 200-pound Oklahoman exploded into prominence as a member of Notre Dame's Killer Bee Backfield. He rushed for 1,343 yards in 1992, the third highest single-season total in school history, and scored 14 touchdowns for a 10-1-1 team. The brother and teammate of Tony Brooks rushed for 1,508 career yards and averaged a Notre Dame-record 7.6 per carry.

JEROME BETTIS
1990-92

He was the pounder in Notre Dame's Killer Bee Backfield, a punishing touchdown-making machine for three college seasons. Before the 6-foot, 247-pound Bettis left school a year early to begin his outstanding NFL career, he managed to rush for 1,912 yards and score 33 TDs (running and receiving) for teams that won 29 games. Bettis was a sophomore in 1991 when he rushed for 972 yards, caught passes for 190 and scored a school-record 120 points.

JEFF BURRIS
1990-93

The versatile and athletic Burris made four-year contributions on both sides of the ball and special teams. As a safety and cornerback, he made 10 interceptions and 189 tackles; as a runner used primarily in goal-line situations, he averaged 4.7 yards and scored 10 TDs; as a return man, he totaled 419 yards and scored once. Burris was a consensus All-American free safety and captain in 1993 when the 11-1 Irish barely missed winning a national title.

AARON TAYLOR
1990-93

The massive 6-4, 299-pound offensive guard/tackle was a junior and senior consensus All-American for teams that posted a 21-2-1 record. Taylor was dominating and smart, whether protecting his quarterback or clearing traffic for Notre Dame runners as a three-year starter. He was a senior captain, winner of the Lombardi Award (the nation's top college lineman) and one of three finalists for the Outland Trophy.

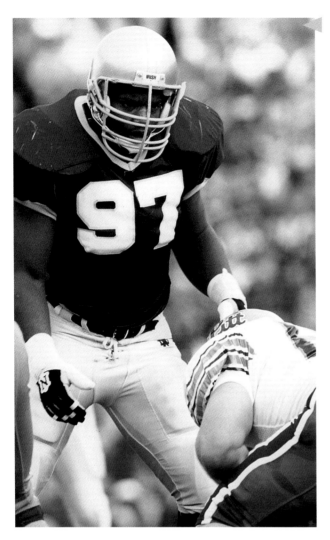

BRYANT YOUNG 1990-93

Few blockers could match up one-on-one against the 6-3, 277-pound Young, who thrived as a three-year starter at defensive tackle. The rugged Chicagoan led the Fighting Irish in sacks (13½) and tackles for lost yardage over his junior and senior seasons and started the final 26 games of his college career. Young, a captain on the 1993 team that finished 11-1, is still active in the NFL.

BOBBY TAYLOR 1992-94

The two-time All-American (consensus as a junior) left Notre Dame after three seasons to begin his outstanding NFL career. The athletic 6-3, 201-pound Texan was a gifted cover cornerback, an aggressive run supporter and a leader for teams that posted 10-1-1 and 11-1 records in his freshman and sophomore campaigns. Taylor made only five interceptions, a reflection of opponents' refusal to throw in his area.

DERRICK MAYES 1992-95

Only three Notre Dame players caught more passes; nobody piled up more reception yardage (2,512) than the 6-1, 204-pound Indianapolis native. Mayes, who averaged 19.4 yards per catch over four seasons, had sure hands and breakaway speed, which helped him produce a school-record 22 receiving touchdowns. Mayes caught 48 passes as a senior captain and scored TDs on 39- and 33-yard passes in a 31-26 loss to Florida State in the 1996 Orange Bowl.

RON POWLUS 1994-97

Notre Dame's career leader in completions (558), passing yards (7,602) and touchdown passes (52) was a four-year starter and two-time captain for teams that posted a 30-17-1 record. The 6-2, 225-pound Powlus, who redshirted in 1993 because of an injury, threw for 1,729 yards and a school-record 19 TDs as a freshman in 1994 and 1,942 yards and 12 TDs while leading a 1996 team that averaged 463.7 yards and 37 points per game.

AUTRY DENSON 1995-98

The 5-10, 200-pound speedster owns the Notre Dame record for career rushing yards (4,318) and finished his career with 47 total touchdowns and a 5-yard per carry average. Denson, the second Fighting Irish player to post three 1,000-yard rushing seasons, reached the 100-yard plateau 22 times for teams that posted a 33-15 record. He ran for 130 yards and three TDs in a 35-28 loss to Georgia Tech in the 1999 Gator Bowl.

JARIOUS JACKSON 1996-99

A backup to Ron Powlus for two seasons, the 6-1, 228-pounder was a double-threat quarterback in the Tony Rice mold. Jackson passed for 1,740 yards and ran for 441 more as a junior and set a single-season school passing record with 2,753 yards in 1999 for a 5-7 team. The strong, physical performer from Tupelo, Miss., a senior captain under coach Bob Davie, finished his career with 34 touchdown passes.

SHANE WALTON 1999-2002

The former walk-on began his Notre Dame career as a freshman soccer sensation and ended it in 2002 as a consensus All-American cornerback. Walton, who scored 10 goals for the Irish soccer team in 1998, switched to football in '99 and became a defensive starter in 2000 for the 9-3 Irish. Athletic and lightning quick, the 5-11 Californian intercepted 11 career passes—seven (two for TDs) in a spectacular final season.

MEMORABLE MOMENTS

WINNING ONE FOR THE GIPPER

1

"When things are wrong and the breaks are beating the boys, tell them to go in there with all they've got and win just one for the Gipper." So legendary Notre Dame player George Gipp, speaking from his deathbed in 1920, told Fighting Irish coach Knute Rockne. Eight years later, with the Irish taking on Army and enduring what for Notre Dame was a down season (a 4-2 record), Rockne exhorted his players by telling them "this is the day and you are the team." The occasion was the 15th meeting of the Irish and the Cadets, the date was November 10, 1928, and the place was Yankee Stadium. Gipp had asked Rockne to implore his squad in the face of a "hopeless" situation—and, in view of Army's 6-0 record and injury-riddled Notre Dame's middling performance to date, this game seemed to qualify. Strangely, there is some debate whether Rockne delivered the mother of all pep talks just before the game or at halftime, when the teams were engaged in a 0-0 deadlock. But inspired his troops were, even though they fell behind, 6-0. Notre Dame struck on Jack Chevigny's one-yard touchdown run and on a 32-yard pass from John Niemiec to little-used Johnny O'Brien and held on for a 12-6 victory, an edge-of-the-seat triumph assured only when the final gun sounded with Army perched on the Notre Dame 1-yard line. The Irish would finish the '28 season at 5-4—no, it wasn't the stuff of Irish lore. But what occurred inside the locker room at Yankee Stadium that day in November surely was.

Inspiration was delivered in many ways by the incomparable Knute Rockne, whose well-documented powers of persuasion were not limited to locker room oratory.

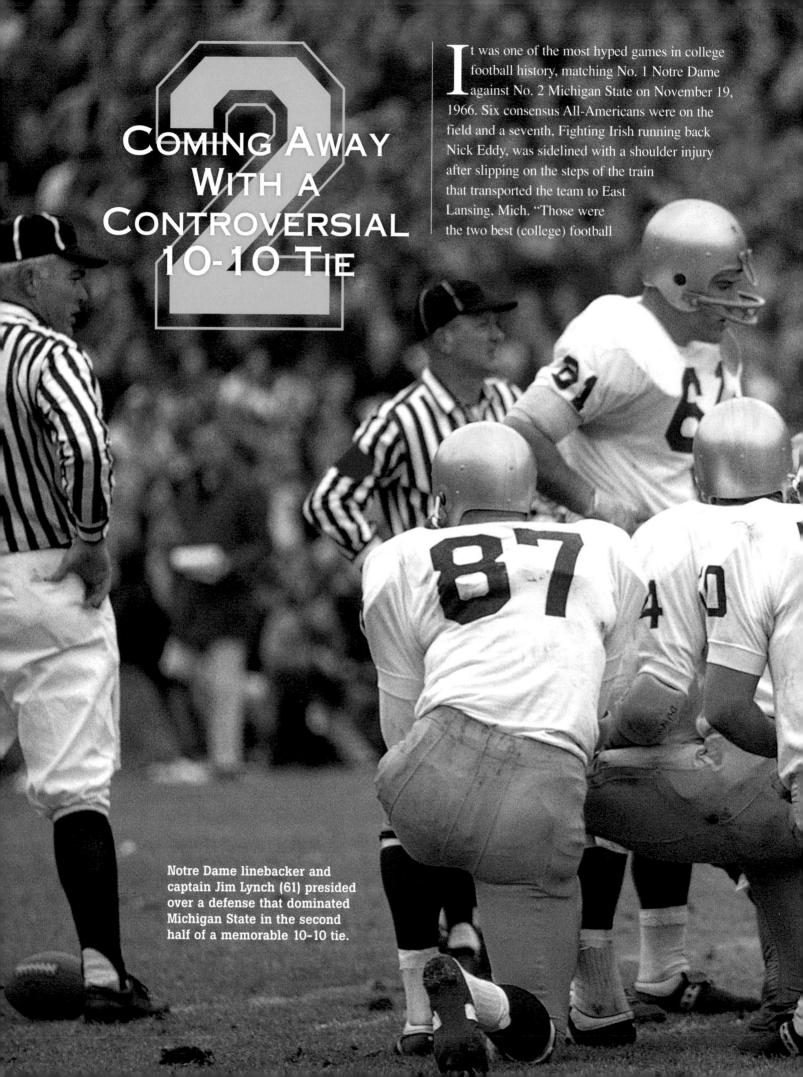

COMING AWAY WITH A CONTROVERSIAL 10-10 TIE

It was one of the most hyped games in college football history, matching No. 1 Notre Dame against No. 2 Michigan State on November 19, 1966. Six consensus All-Americans were on the field and a seventh, Fighting Irish running back Nick Eddy, was sidelined with a shoulder injury after slipping on the steps of the train that transported the team to East Lansing, Mich. "Those were the two best (college) football

Notre Dame linebacker and captain Jim Lynch (61) presided over a defense that dominated Michigan State in the second half of a memorable 10-10 tie.

teams ever to play each other," Irish quarterback Terry Hanratty said with conviction decades later. Ara Parseghian's squad was forced to overcome another key injury when Hanratty suffered a shoulder separation in the first quarter on a hit by Bubba Smith and George Webster. Minus considerable offensive firepower and with star receiver Jim Seymour unable to snare a pass all day, Notre Dame found itself in a hole—one made only deeper when Michigan State shot ahead, 10-0, in the second quarter. Coley O'Brien, who replaced Hanratty, rallied the Irish with a 34-yard touchdown pass to Bob Gladieux later in that quarter, and Notre Dame drew even at 10-10 at the outset of the fourth quarter on Joe Azzaro's 28-yard field goal. With 1:24 to play

and positioned at their own 30, the Irish proceeded to run the ball three times—shockingly, Parseghian seemed content with a tie. Notre Dame did gamble on fourth-and-one, and O'Brien sneaked two yards. Apparently hoping to pass on the ensuing play, O'Brien was thrown for a seven-yard loss. Finally, with 6 seconds to go, the quarterback ran to the Irish 39 and time expired. Parseghian defended his play-it-safe strategy in the landmark tie, reasoning that a No. 1 team must be beaten if it is to fall from the top ranking. Associated Press pollsters agreed, but United Press International voters made the Spartans No. 1—for one week, anyway. After Notre Dame crushed Southern California, 51-0, both final polls crowned the Irish as national champions.

TERRELL'S MIGHTY KNOCKDOWN

threw for 424 yards (at the time, a record figure for a Notre Dame opponent), and recovered four Miami fumbles. Quarterback Tony Rice ran for one TD and

Sixty-one points had been scored in the titanic October 15, 1988, struggle between the top-ranked Miami (Fla.) Hurricanes and No. 4 Notre Dame. But it all came down to a two-point conversion attempt by the Hurricanes with 45 seconds remaining at frenzied Notre Dame Stadium. Miami, boasting a 36-game regular-season winning streak and just plain boasting in the eyes of many fans who had grown tired of the Hurricanes' showmanship over the years, had trailed the Fighting Irish, 31-24, in the final minute when Hurricanes quarterback Steve Walsh threw his fourth touchdown pass of the game. With the score now 31-30, Walsh aimed a cross-field pass toward the right corner of the end zone, hoping for a completion that would account for the game's decisive two points. But Notre Dame safety Pat Terrell leaped high and batted the ball safely to the ground. It was a delirious moment for the undefeated Fighting Irish, who after covering a last-gasp onside kick found themselves in solid contention for the national championship. They had upset a Miami team that had routed Notre Dame in the teams' last four meetings (24-0, 58-7, 31-13, 20-0) and one that had infuriated the Irish earlier in the day by running through their pregame calisthenics formation. "We went back to the locker room and vowed not to take anything from them today," said tailback Mark Green, one of Notre Dame's three captains. "They were arrogant and cocky—but they also were very good. They carried that air of confidence and could back it up." Terrell and the Irish played with confidence, too. Terrell also came up big earlier in the game, scoring on a 60-yard interception return. The Irish picked off three passes against Walsh, who

Safety Pat Terrell (15) bats away a two-point conversion pas

passed for another for Notre Dame, which built 21-7 and 31-21 leads and held on for dear life. A big play occurred with seven minutes remaining when Cleveland Gary took a short pass from Walsh to the Irish 1, only to fumble the ball away to Notre Dame's Michael Stonebreaker.

rom Miami quarterback Steve Walsh, ensuring Notre Dame's dramatic 31-30 upset win over the No. 1-ranked Hurricanes.

VAULTING FROM NO. 5 TO NO. 1 IN COTTON BOWL

The Texas Longhorns stood at the head of the college football class as 1977 drew to a close. They were ranked No. 1 in the wire-service polls at the end of the regular season. They were the only unbeaten team left standing among the nation's major colleges. They had the best player in the land, Heisman Trophy winner Earl Campbell. And they had the opportunity to sew up the national championship in their own back yard, a familiar patch of green known as the Cotton Bowl. The Longhorns' opponent for the January 2, 1978, game in Dallas would be No. 5 Notre Dame, which was riding a nine-game winning streak after losing to Mississippi. Dan Devine's Fighting Irish would need at least a little luck of the Irish to get past the mighty 'Horns and more than a little luck to realize their still-flickering national-title aspirations. But the Irish eschewed luck in favor of a sure thing—a hard-hitting, alert defense that gave the Notre Dame offense the ball in prime Texas real estate. The Fighting Irish converted the first five of six Longhorn turnovers into scores, with three fumble recoveries and two interceptions giving them the ball on Texas' 32-, 27-, 35-, 20- and 29-yard lines. The Irish, who never trailed, jumped to a 24-3 lead and wound up 38-10 winners. Notre Dame's Vagas Ferguson rushed for 100 yards and two touchdowns and also scored on a 17-yard pass from Joe Montana. Terry Eurick had two TD runs for Notre Dame and Jerome Heavens ran for 101 yards (second-best to Campbell's 116 for Texas). It was an astonishingly convincing triumph for the Irish, one that convinced final AP and UPI pollsters that Notre Dame was No. 1.

Terry Eurick (40) celebrates one of his two touchdown runs

...and Irish coach Dan Devine revels (inset) after a championship-sealing 38-10 win over No. 1 Texas in the Cotton Bowl.

ENDING OKLAHOMA'S 47-GAME WINNING STREAK

Coming off a 2-8 record in 1956, the worst to date in school history, Notre Dame won its first four games in 1957 before regressing. The Fighting Irish lost at home to Navy, 20-6, in Week 5 and then fumbled the ball away five times in an embarrassing 34-6 setback at Michigan State. Up next was college football's reigning behemoth, Oklahoma, which had just extended its record major-college winning streak to 47 games with a 39-14 thumping of Missouri. The talented, deep and extremely well-conditioned Sooners had dealt Notre Dame its worst-ever home defeat in '56, a 40-0 drubbing, and Bud Wilkinson's team would now get the Irish on its home turf in Norman, Okla., on November 16. Oklahoma, which had scored in 123 consecutive games, marched down the field on its first possession and reached the Irish 13-yard line before stalling. The Sooners would get no closer to the end zone the rest of the day as the game evolved into a taut defensive struggle. Terry Brennan's Notre Dame team demonstrated it could move the ball, and the Irish put together a sustained drive in the fourth quarter that culminated in a fourth-and-goal play from the Oklahoma 3. With the Sooners' defense stacked up in anticipation of a blast into the line by Irish fullback Nick Pietrosante, Bob Williams (the second Notre Dame quarterback with that name) faked to Pietrosante, rolled to the right and pitched out to halfback Dick Lynch, whose dash into the end zone with 3:50 remaining capped an 80-yard march. Monty Stickles followed with the conversion kick, and the Irish—getting an end-zone interception from Williams with 22 seconds to play—made the 7-0 score hold up. The remarkable streak was history.

With the Oklahoma defense focusing on Fighting Irish fullback Nick Pietrosante, Dick Lynch (25) heads for the end zone with a Bob Williams pitch and the only touchdown in a streak-ending upset of the powerful Sooners. The stunning outcome earned coach Terry Brennan a victory ride (inset).

CLEMENTS-TO-WEBER COMPLETION WINS NATIONAL TITLE

Trying desperately to hold on to a 24-23 lead over top-ranked Alabama in the late going of the December 31, 1973, Sugar Bowl, Notre Dame faced a third-and-eight play from its 3-yard line. The Fighting Irish, ranked No. 3 in the AP poll, knew they couldn't play conservatively—being forced to punt undoubtedly would give Bear Bryant's Crimson Tide excellent field position and an opportunity to kick a game-winning field goal. But the Irish really couldn't afford to gamble, either—a turnover would be just just as calamitous. Coach Ara Parseghian, who had been heavily criticized seven years earlier for his close-to-the-vest play-calling in Notre Dame's 10-10 tie with Michigan State, took a different approach this time. His directive passed along to quarterback Tom Clements, Parseghian watched anxiously from the sideline as the play began to unfold from a two-tight-end set. Clements retreated into his end zone and looked for his main target, tight end Dave Casper. Instead, he fired the ball downfield toward No. 2 tight end Robin Weber, who was wide open. Weber latched on to the pass for a 35-yard gain. Notre Dame not only had clinched the victory—the Fighting Irish proceeded to run out the clock—but the Irish had wrapped up another national championship, the AP making it official three days later when it released its final poll. (Alabama was voted No. 1 by UPI, which completed its balloting before the bowl games.) Notre Dame, at 11-0, was unbeaten and untied for the first time since 1949. Clements' stellar play in the Sugar Bowl—his 30-yard strike to Casper on another third-down play in the fourth quarter had set up a decisive field goal—

put the Irish over the top. But he had plenty of help in New Orleans. Al Hunter returned a kickoff 93 yards for a touchdown, Wayne Bullock and Eric Penick rushed for TDs and Bob Thomas drilled the winning 19-yard field goal with 4:26 to play. And

Parseghian, on the daring pass play that clinched the victory, made what Clements referred to as a "great call—nobody was expecting it." No one was expecting Weber to make the big catch, that's for sure. It was his only reception of the entire season.

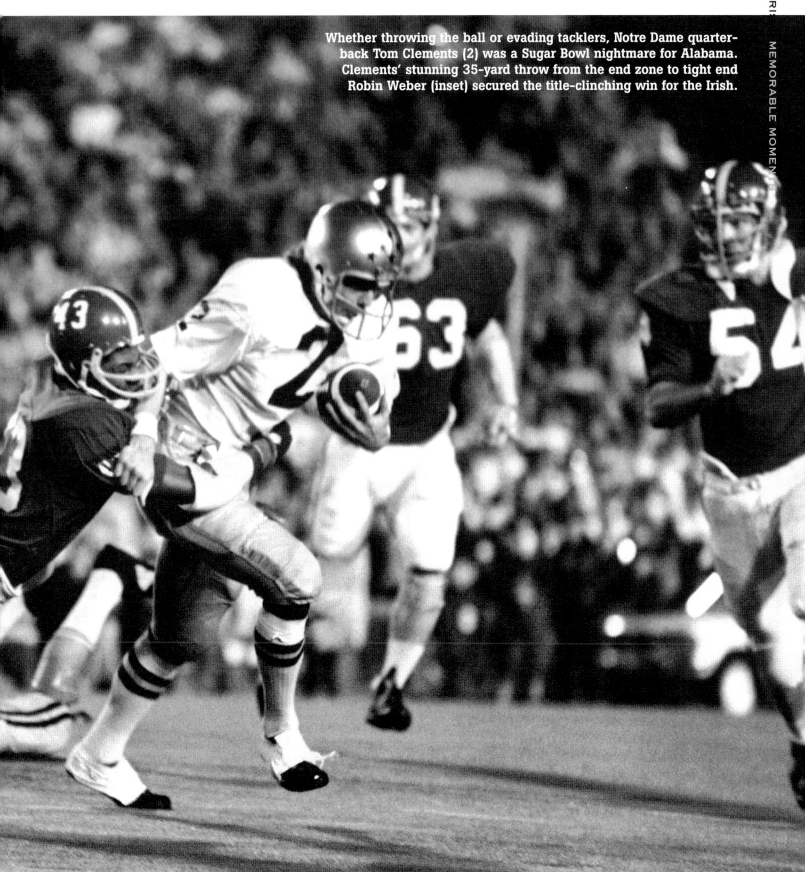

Whether throwing the ball or evading tacklers, Notre Dame quarterback Tom Clements (2) was a Sugar Bowl nightmare for Alabama. Clements' stunning 35-yard throw from the end zone to tight end Robin Weber (inset) secured the title-clinching win for the Irish.

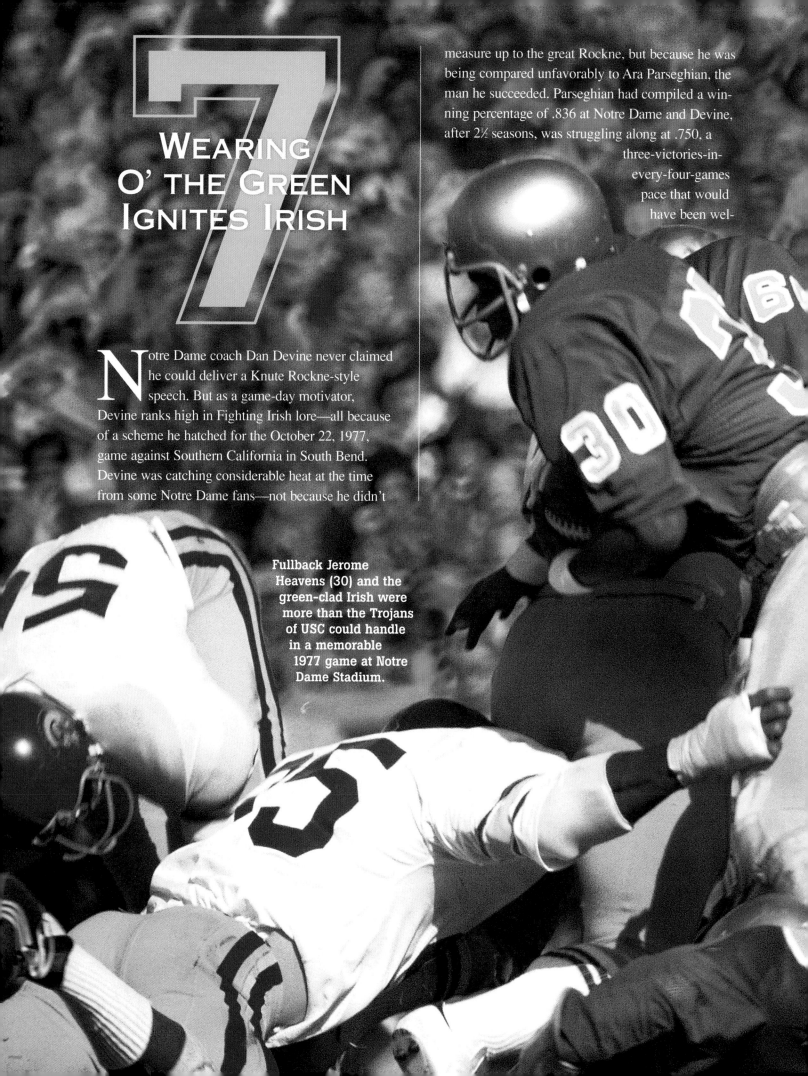

7
WEARING O' THE GREEN IGNITES IRISH

N otre Dame coach Dan Devine never claimed he could deliver a Knute Rockne-style speech. But as a game-day motivator, Devine ranks high in Fighting Irish lore—all because of a scheme he hatched for the October 22, 1977, game against Southern California in South Bend. Devine was catching considerable heat at the time from some Notre Dame fans—not because he didn't measure up to the great Rockne, but because he was being compared unfavorably to Ara Parseghian, the man he succeeded. Parseghian had compiled a winning percentage of .836 at Notre Dame and Devine, after 2½ seasons, was struggling along at .750, a three-victories-in-every-four-games pace that would have been wel-

Fullback Jerome Heavens (30) and the green-clad Irish were more than the Trojans of USC could handle in a memorable 1977 game at Notre Dame Stadium.

comed at most institutions. Many of Devine's critics also considered him unimaginative—but little did they know. Before the USC game in '77, Devine sent the Fighting Irish onto the field for warmups in their usual dark-blue jerseys. But when they returned to the dressing room, green jerseys were hanging in their lockers.

Already fired up because they were playing the archrival Trojans in a battle of once-beaten teams, the Fighting Irish felt an adrenaline rush when they saw the green tops, a ploy Devine had managed to keep secret. When Notre Dame returned to the field, fans erupted in wild celebration—and neither the Fighting Irish nor their faithful could be contained the rest of the day. Notre Dame, paced by Joe Montana's two touchdown passes and two one-yard TD runs, dismantled the Trojans, 49-19, at raucous Notre Dame Stadium and went on to win the national title. It was a championship run that almost certainly began on the October day that the 1977 Irish showed their true colors.

SOUTHERN CAL. OCT. 22, 1977

Sec. 18 Row 37 Seat 28

RESERVED SEAT $10.00

LUJACK'S TACKLE SAVES TIE WITH ARMY

Statistically, Notre Dame quarterback Johnny Lujack had a bad day in one of the greatest college football games of all time—the 1946 battle between the second-ranked Fighting Irish and No. 1 Army, winner of 25 consecutive games. Lujack completed only 6-of-17 passes for 52 yards and was intercepted three times. Plus, he carried the ball eight times and made a mere nine yards. But on a day when gifted offensive players on both squads were held in check and the teams dueled to a 0-0 tie, Lujack nonetheless made the game's big play—on the other side of the ball. Army's Doc Blanchard, limited to 50 yards on 18 rushing attempts, got the Yankee Stadium crowd off its collective feet in the third quarter when he broke into the clear and headed downfield—only to be brought down by Lujack's open-field tackle at the Notre Dame 37-yard line. Conventional wisdom said the Cadets' Mr. Inside could not be stopped one-on-one when he saw daylight, but Lujack proved the experts wrong. Shortly after Blanchard's run—which covered 21 yards—Terry Brennan also came up big for the Fighting Irish. Brennan snuffed out Army's threat by picking off a Glenn Davis pass at the Irish 8. Notre Dame, which had been overwhelmed by Army (59-0 and 48-0) the previous two seasons while Frank Leahy was serving in the Navy, stood shoulder to shoulder with the Cadets in the coach's first year back. And although Army and Notre Dame still ranked 1-2 in the AP poll released the week after their momentous November 9 clash, the Fighting Irish had shown their mettle—and by season's end they slipped past Earl "Red" Blaik's team in the ratings. Clearly, no one could say Lujack's play and the scoreless deadlock mattered naught.

Notre Dame defender Emil Sitko intercepts an Army pass as Johnny Lujack (32) looks for a carom. It was Lujack who saved the 0-0 tie with a dramatic one-on-one tackle of end zone-bound Army runner Doc Blanchard.

IRISH DREAM FLUTTERS AWAY ON EAGLES' LATE FIELD GOAL

Just how much excitement—downright frenzy, really—could venerable Notre Dame Stadium take? Just the week before, No. 2 Notre Dame had wrested away the No. 1 ranking from Florida State in a tumultuous 31-24 win over the Seminoles, a game that wasn't officially added to the "W" column until Fighting Irish cornerback Shawn Wooden batted down an end zone-bound pass as the clock ran out. Now, on November 20, 1993, the stadium was sheer bedlam as Irish fans reveled in one of the great comebacks in Notre Dame history. Trailing Boston College 38-17 with about 11 minutes remaining in the fourth quarter, the Irish went on a 22-0 spree in the next 10 minutes. Lou Holtz's team seized the lead for the first time with 1:09 to play when Kevin Pendergast booted a conversion kick after a four-yard touchdown pass from Kevin McDougal to Lake Dawson. Considering the teams had moved the ball at will most of the day—they combined for more than 900 yards in total offense—Notre Dame's 39-38 lead, while a wondrous accomplishment, was no sure thing. Boston College, playing with confidence and riding a seven-game winning streak after starting the season with two losses, appeared fully capable of creating its own mayhem in the final 69 seconds—and the Eagles got a helping hand when the Irish were assessed a 15-yard personal-foul penalty after stopping BC at its 10-yard line on the kickoff. Quarterback Glenn Foley's four completions drove Boston College to the Notre Dame 24, from where left-footed kicker David Gordon attempted a 41-yard field goal. The knuckleball-like kick sailed long and true as time expired, and Notre Dame's No. 1 ranking and national-championship hopes sailed away with it in a wrenching 41-39 defeat.

Lake Dawson's four-yard TD reception (above) capped Notre Dame's dramatic comeback against Boston College.
But the Eagles soared last when David Gordon (14, inset) connected on a game-ending 41-yard field goal.

HIGH DRAMA IN COLUMBUS: SHAKESPEARE'S TD PASS

The Associated Press' weekly poll of college football teams was still a year away, but it didn't take a vote of sportswriters and broadcasters to tell fans that the Ohio State Buckeyes and Fighting Irish were among the nation's finest teams in 1935. And on November 2 at Ohio Stadium in Columbus, the 5-0 Irish and 4-0 Buckeyes squared off in a game that captured the imagination of fans from coast to coast, many of whom listened to it on CBS radio. Ohio State jumped to a 13-0 halftime lead and nursed the two-touchdown advantage until early in the fourth quarter when the Irish struck on a short TD run by Steve Miller. Then, with about three minutes remaining, Notre Dame set off on an 80-yard march capped by a 33-yard scoring pass from Andy Pilney to Mike Layden, brother of Irish coach Elmer Layden. Strangely, the Irish still trailed, 13-12, having blown both extra-point attempts. With a minute and a half to play, Ohio State covered an onside kick and merely had to run out the clock. But Pilney forced a fumble when the Buckeyes tried

a thrust into the line, and the Irish recovered the ball at the Ohio State 49. With a throng of 82,000 fans growing ever anxious, Pilney looked to pass but set out on his own when he couldn't locate an open receiver and reached the Buckeyes' 19 before being forced out of bounds—and out of the game with a knee injury. Enter Bill Shakespeare, with about a half-minute to play. Shakespeare was nearly intercepted on his first throw, but he quickly redeemed himself after being fed a play from coach Layden by way of reserve Jim McKenna. A scrub quarterback who didn't rate a place on the Notre Dame traveling squad, McKenna had sneaked aboard the train to Columbus in hopes of being a spectator at the big game but wound up dressing for the showdown once Layden became aware of his grit and resourcefulness. Playing a messenger role, McKenna conveyed the play to Shakespeare, who proceeded to rifle a touchdown strike to Wayne Millner. Pilney, being carried to the dressing room with his injury, was told what the crowd's reaction clearly suggested: Notre Dame had won, by the score of 18-13. Shakespeare had been center stage in this remarkable football drama, one that also will be remembered for a bit part played by an obscure teammate.

Elmer Layden (center), one of Notre Dame's Four Horsemen in 1924, coached the Fighting Irish to their 1935 upset of the Buckeyes.

Bill Shakespeare (below) wrote a cruel ending for Ohio State in the 'Game of the Century.' He got plenty of help from (left to right) Jim McKenna, Andy Pilney and Wayne Millner.

The much-heralded Fighting Irish-Buckeyes battle of 1935 was witnessed by a full house at massive Ohio Stadium.

GREATEST PERFORMANCES

ROCKNE'S 105-12-5 RECORD

1

It is one of the most imposing records ever achieved on any level of athletic competition. Knute Rockne compiled it over 13 seasons as Notre Dame football coach, and the numbers go like this: 105 victories, 12 defeats and five ties. A winning percentage of .881, easily the best figure in NCAA Division I-A history. Five undefeated and untied seasons. Three national championships. Winning streaks of 20, 19, 16 and 14 games. Thirty-four victories in one 35-game stretch; 22 wins in another span of 23 games. One losing streak—Rockne's teams lost two consecutive games only once. His record, year by year:

Season	W	L	T
1918	3	1	2
1919	9	0	0
1920	9	0	0
1921	10	1	0
1922	8	1	1
1923	9	1	0
*1924	10	0	0
1925	7	2	1
1926	9	1	0
1927	7	1	1
1928	5	4	0
*1929	9	0	0
*1930	10	0	0

* National champions.

Knute Rockne, the mentor of Notre Dame football, poses with 1925 team captain Clem Crowe, a two-way end.

THREE NATIONAL TITLES, 36-0-2 RECORD

The records, year by year:

Season	W	L	T
* 1946	8	0	1
* 1947	9	0	0
1948	9	0	1
* 1949	10	0	0

* National champions.

When a university holds the all-time NCAA Division I-A record for winning percentage—as Notre Dame does with a .750 mark—success has come at a dizzying clip. But for sheer dominance of the college football landscape, the Fighting Irish were at their overpowering best from 1946 through 1949, a four-season span in which they put together a 36-0-2 record and won three national championships. In their lone non-title season, 1948, they went unbeaten (with one tie) and finished No. 2 in the country. Frank Leahy was the mastermind of the remarkable unbeaten stretch—a period in which he coached two Heisman Trophy winners (Johnny Lujack in 1947 and Leon Hart in 1949), two Outland Trophy recipients (George Connor in 1946 and Bill Fischer in 1948) and 11 consensus All-American selections. Twenty-eight of Notre Dame's 36 victories were by 20 or more points, and Leahy's Irish outscored their 38 opponents to the tune of 1,242 (32.7 points per game) to 255 (6.7). No team scored more than six points against the 1946 Irish and only one team managed more than seven points against the 1947 squad. From Week 7 of the '46 season through Week 9 of the '48 season, Notre Dame won 21 consecutive games. Keeping Notre Dame from a perfect record over the four years were two of the Irish's fiercest rivals, Army and Southern California. The Cadets played Notre Dame to a memorable 0-0 tie in 1946, and USC managed a 14-14 standoff with Leahy's team in 1948.

Frank Leahy (right) coached the Fighting Irish to four national championships, three in a spectacular run from 1946-49.

Notre Dame's incredible four-year 36-0-2 legacy was carved out by a talented cast of players that included Heisman Trophy winners Johnny Lujack (32) and Leon Hart (82), two-time consensus All-American Emil Sitko (14) and Outland Trophy winner George Connor (81).

THE WILD RIDE OF THE FOUR HORSEMEN

"**O**utlined against a blue-gray October sky, the Four Horsemen rode again. In dramatic lore, they are known as Famine, Pestilence, Destruction and Death. These are only aliases. Their real names are Stuhldreher, Miller, Crowley and Layden. They formed the crest of the South Bend cyclone before which another fighting Army football team was swept over the precipice at the Polo Grounds yesterday afternoon as 55,000 spectators peered down on the bewildering panorama spread on the green plain below." Unquestionably, New York Herald Tribune sportswriter Grantland Rice, describing what he had witnessed on October 18, 1924, was in awe of Notre Dame's backfield, which had just turned in the greatest of its many superlative performances over a three-year period. Halfbacks Don Miller and Jim Crowley and fullback Elmer Layden combined for 310 yards rushing and quarterback Harry Stuhldreher ran the Fighting Irish offense with precision as Notre Dame defeated Army, 13-7. Miller and Crowley were unstoppable, the former gaining 148 yards on 19 carries and the latter 102 on 17 attempts. Layden ran one yard for a second-quarter touchdown and Crowley went 20 for a third-quarter TD. For the season, Miller, a constant breakaway threat, rushed for 763 yards, Crowley 739 and Layden 423. Stuhldreher completed 75.8 percent of his passes in 1924, hitting on 25-of-33 attempts. Notre Dame swept through the regular season undefeated, then capped a 10-0 run with a 27-10 triumph over Stanford in the Rose Bowl, a game in which Layden scored twice on long interception returns and also ran for a TD. The Four Horsemen

had come together as a unit late in the 1922 season, and they flourished in 1923 when Notre Dame went 9-1. Only Nebraska was able to slow the Horsemen's gait, handing Notre Dame its only

defeats in '22 and '23. Stuhldreher promised a pay-back against the Cornhuskers in 1924—and he and his teammates delivered, as a 34-6 Irish triumph would attest.

The talented 1924 backfield of (left to right) Don Miller, Elmer Layden, Jim Crowley and Harry Stuhldreher was immortalized by sportswriter Grantland Rice as the Four Horsemen.

THE ULTIMATE ROADSHOW

Winning a national championship is difficult under any circumstances. But trying to win one without playing a single game at home seems impossible—even for a renowned program under the guidance of an extraordinary coach. Notre Dame and Knute Rockne faced just such a task in 1929, a year in which the Fighting Irish would play all nine of their games away from South Bend because excavation was under way on campus for a gleaming new stadium. The phrase "challenging schedule" took on new meaning for the Irish, who faced this daunting road in the fall of '29 after enduring a four-loss season in 1928:

DATE	OPPONENT	SITE
October 5	Indiana	Bloomington
October 12	Navy	Baltimore
October 19	Wisconsin	Chicago
October 26	Carnegie Tech	Pittsburgh
November 2	Georgia Tech	Atlanta
November 9	Drake	Chicago
November 16	Southern Calif.	Chicago
November 23	Northwestern	Evanston, Ill.
November 30	Army	New York

The three games in Chicago and the contests in Baltimore and New York were listed as neutral-site games, although a case could be made that Navy was playing in its own back yard in Baltimore and Army was right at home in New York's Yankee Stadium. Still, Notre Dame, with its widespread fan base and subway alumni, was highly popular in both venues. Whatever the obstacles, the Fighting Irish were up to the job—even with Rockne spending considerable time away from the team because of poor health. Notre Dame's rock-ribbed defense held the nine opponents to 38 points and the offense, led by consensus All-American quarterback

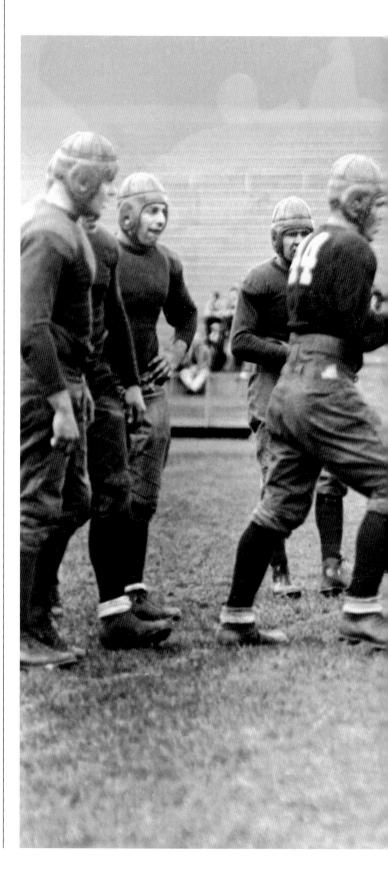

Frank Carideo and fullback Joe Savoldi, was efficient enough to enable Notre Dame to run the table. The Irish defeated Indiana, 14-0; Navy, 14-7; Wisconsin, 19-0; Carnegie Tech, 7-0; Georgia Tech, 26-6; Drake, 19-7; Southern California, 13-12; Northwestern, 26-6, and Army, 7-0. It added up to a 9-0 roadshow and, yes, a national championship.

There was, literally, no place like home for Knute Rockne and his 1929 Fighting Irish, who played (and won) all nine of their scheduled games on the road en route to an unlikely and unprecedented national championship.

MIRACLE COMEBACK IN 1979 COTTON BOWL

The temperature in Dallas was in the 20s and the wind was swirling. More than half of the ticket-holders for the January 1, 1979, Cotton Bowl stayed at home, and midway through the fourth quarter you couldn't blame Joe Montana for wishing he had stayed inside, too. Notre Dame was trailing Houston, 34-12, and the Fighting Irish quarterback, nursing a cold and a touch of the flu, had thrown three interceptions. A year removed from their rousing 38-10 victory over Texas in the same bowl game—a win that catapulted them to the national championship—the Irish appeared spent this time around. But not so fast. Notre Dame's Tony Belden proceeded to block a Houston punt, and Steve Cichy gathered up the loose ball and sped 33 yards for an Irish touchdown. Montana hit Vagas Ferguson with a two-point conversion pass and, with 7:25 to play, Notre Dame had moved within 34-20. The Cougars stalled on the ensuing drive and the Irish took over at their own 39 after forcing a punt.

Montana's deft passing highlighted a quick five-play drive, a march capped by his two-yard TD run and second straight two-point conversion completion (this one to Kris Haines). It was now 34-28, and there was still 4:15 remaining. The teams then exchanged possessions, Houston being forced to punt and Notre Dame turning the ball over on what seemed to be a game-deciding fumble by Montana. But the Irish would get yet another chance. With 35 seconds remaining, Houston gambled on a fourth-and-one at the Cougars' 29 — and Irish freshman Joe

Quarterback Joe Montana (3, above) engineered the comeback win over Houston, which sparked a celebration by Kris Haines (82, right) after he caught the climactic TD pass with no time remaining.

Gramke stopped Emmett King for no gain. Montana then scrambled for 11 yards and threw to Haines for 10 more. The Irish were now on the Houston 8 with six seconds on the clock. Montana again went to Haines, this time failing to connect.

Two seconds remained. Montana to Haines, one more time ... touchdown! With no time showing on the clock, Joe Unis kicked the extra point—not once, but twice (because of an Irish penalty). Notre Dame 35, Houston 34.

ISMAIL'S RETURN FEAT IS WORTHY OF AN ENCORE

Raghib Ismail (25), Notre Dame's 'Rocket,' gets a warm sideline reception from teammates after the second of two kickoff-return touchdowns (inset) during a 1989 game at Michigan Stadium. It was the second time Ismail had performed the two-in-one feat.

"It doesn't matter who's back there, if you have guys who block and know all their assignments. Anyone can do it, to tell you the truth." So said Notre Dame freshman Raghib Ismail on November 5, 1988, explaining to sportswriters how he was able to return two kickoffs for touchdowns against Rice that afternoon. A more plausible explanation surely could be found in Ismail's nickname: Rocket. The man could fly. Plus, he was tough and had the knack of taking away the angles of would-be tacklers. Ismail broke two tackles against the Owls on his first TD sprint, which covered 87 yards, and he traveled 83 yards on his second return for a score as unbeaten Notre Dame punished winless Rice, 54-11, at Notre Dame Stadium. A little more than 10 months later, Ismail, a 5-10, 175-pound flanker who had been clocked with 4.28 speed over 40 yards, defied the odds by reprising the runback feat. In a September 16, 1989, game between No. 1 Notre Dame and No. 2 Michigan in Ann Arbor, he gathered up the second-half kickoff and streaked 88 yards to a touchdown—no small feat against the Wolverines, who hadn't allowed a kickoff-return TD in 32 years. Then, in the fourth quarter, Ismail covered 92 yards on a kickoff, the touchdown muting a Michigan rally led by quarterback Elvis Grbac, who was making his college debut in a relief role. The Fighting Irish won, 24-19. Ismail's feat of twice returning two kickoffs for TDs in one game is unequaled in the history of major-college football.

HUARTE'S STORYBOOK 1964 SEASON

John Huarte wanted to earn his first letter in 1964—his senior season at Notre Dame. Slowed by injuries, he had thrown only eight passes as a sophomore. As a junior, he had played just 42 minutes in what proved to be a long season—the Fighting Irish finished 2-7 and Huarte, again, was excluded from the lettermen's club. So, the quarterback had one last season to make his mark. And make it he did—incredibly, he won the Heisman Trophy. Huarte's believe-it-or-not story began to take shape in the spring of '64 when, with new coach Ara Parseghian looking on, he showed skill in setting up to pass and demonstrated a quick release. Then, over the summer, Huarte and Irish teammate/fellow Californian Jack Snow, a wingback-turned-receiver, worked long hours on their pass-catch technique and timing. Parseghian, though not thrilled with Huarte's three-quarters (sometimes sidearm) delivery, was willing to give him a chance that fall—a decision made, in part, because of Notre Dame's shallow depth chart. In the season opener at Wisconsin, Huarte and Snow teamed up on 61- and 42-yard touchdown passes. Huarte followed with two TD passes against Purdue, then threw for two scores and ran for two touchdowns against Air Force. Against UCLA, Huarte and Snow combined for their fifth TD in four games. The next week, Huarte threw for 300 yards against Stanford. He followed with three touchdown strikes against Navy, a game in which he hit on only 10 passes but averaged 27.4 yards per completion. In Week 7, Huarte and Nick Eddy combined on a 91-yard scoring pass at Pittsburgh. After playing a superlative all-around game

Fighting Irish quarterback John Huarte throws a 1964 pass

against Michigan State, Huarte shrugged off wintry conditions the following week and jolted Iowa with a 66-yard TD pass to Snow. While Huarte was resurrecting his career, Parseghian was doing the same for Notre Dame football. The Irish were unbeaten and ranked No. 1 entering the season finale at Southern California. And not even an ago-nizing 20-17 loss to the Trojans (a game in which Huarte threw for 272 yards and Snow caught his ninth TD pass) could diminish what Huarte had contributed in 1964—16 touchdown passes, 2,062 aerial yards and a storybook rise from unknown player to Heisman Trophy winner. Oh, yes, he won a letter, too.

against Air Force, a game in which he fired two touchdown passes and ran for two more TDs.

PICKING APART THE WISHBONE

Notre Dame was still a stranger to this bowl-game stuff. Only a year earlier, the university's administration had lifted a 45-year ban on postseason play, a decision that enabled the Irish to accept a bid to play No. 1 Texas in the 1970 Cotton Bowl. The Irish lost that game on a late Longhorns touchdown, but fate—in the form of the Cotton Bowl invitation committee—gave Notre Dame another crack at Texas. The Cotton Bowl of January 1, 1971, would again match a Joe Theismann-led Notre Dame team against a Texas squad that stood atop the national rankings. This time, the Irish faced a Longhorns team boasting a 30-game winning streak—and one with a wishbone attack that had accounted for 374.5 yards rushing per game in the regular season. Notre Dame was no slouch, either—it ranked No. 5 in the UPI poll and No. 6 in the AP rankings and was 9-0 until losing to Southern California in its regular-season finale. Devising a defense that he said mirrored Texas' wishbone, Irish coach Ara Parseghian had his secondary and middle linebacker keying on the Longhorns' running backs— in effect, daring the 'Horns to throw the ball. While the Irish defense picked at the wishbone— Texas ran for 216 yards, down 158.5 from its average—Theismann steered Notre Dame to a 21-3 lead in the first 16½ minutes. The senior quarterback passed 26 yards to Tom Gatewood and ran three yards for first-quarter touchdowns and added a 15-yard TD run in the second quarter. Notre Dame led at halftime, 24-11, and that score held up the rest of the day as the defenses took over. The Irish stuffed Texas' Jim Bertelsen—he made five

yards on eight carries—and held Steve Worster to 42 yards on 16 attempts. Longhorns quarterback Eddie Phillips passed for 199 yards and ran for 164 more, but his totals were more than offset by the poor numbers put up by Worster and Bertelsen—

and the fact Texas lost the ball on five of its nine fumbles. Notre Dame jumped to No. 2 in the final AP poll, with Nebraska supplanting Texas at the top. UPI, which released its final poll before the bowl games, listed the Longhorns as No. 1.

Joe Theismann (7), always armed and dangerous, used his legs to score a first-quarter Cotton Bowl touchdown against Texas en route to a Notre Dame upset that ended the Longhorns' 30-game winning streak.

Prominence for the Irish and the Passing Game

Notre Dame had something to prove when it ventured to West Point for a November 1, 1913, game with Army. It wound up making two points—and doing so with a flair. Most of all, the Fighting Irish wanted to show they could compete with college football's big boys. Sure, the Irish had compiled a 44-3-5 record over the previous seven years, but a significant percentage of the victories had come against small colleges from the Midwest. Of course, Notre Dame itself was a "small Catholic school in the Midwest"—but one with big-time ambitions when it came to its football program. The Army game offered a perfect showcase for coach Jesse Harper's team, which knew the East was the reigning power base of college football and that the Eastern press would prove a tough critic when judging the wares of an upstart from another region. Army jumped ahead, 13-7—the Irish had scored on a pass from quarterback Gus Dorais to end Knute Rockne, who feigned a limp and lulled his defender to sleep—but the Cadets were outscored, 28-0, the rest of the way as Notre Dame befuddled Army defenders with its aerial game. Previously, most college teams passed the ball only in desperate situations, but Notre Dame was throwing it as an integral part of its offense. Whenever Army defenders crashed the line in hopes of stopping a running play, Dorais dumped the ball off. Or he would connect with Rockne on a precision pass play, hitting his receiver in full stride. And when Army spread its defense in an attempt to extend its pass coverage, Notre Dame's backs reeled off huge chunks of yardage. Dorais wound up with the then-

phenomenal total of 243 passing yards, and Notre Dame wound up with a 35-13 victory. It was a game that made believers (Eastern press included) out of those who questioned the legitimacy of the Irish as a big-time player in college football. And it won converts to the forward pass, which had been legalized in college football seven years earlier but never exploited the way it was on this day.

Army players chase Notre Dame end Knute Rockne (right), the target of a Gus Dorais touchdown pass in a 1913 game at West Point. Dorais (inset) passed for a then-phenomenal total of 243 yards in the Fighting Irish's 35-13 milestone victory.

THEISMANN'S 526-YARD PASSING DAY

10

ing runs for the Irish, who managed only 31 yards on the ground. Theismann threw four interceptions—only one led directly to a score, a 19-yard field goal—and lost a fumble in the end zone that USC turned into a touchdown. Nonetheless, he put on an amazing show—one *The New York Times* called a "spectacular performance" that resulted in a "far-fetched total of 526 yards." Considering the importance of the game and Theismann's efforts to pull it out, the defeat was particularly galling to Irish fans, who remembered all too well that six years earlier (to the day) Notre Dame had seen a perfect season and dreams of a national title end in a loss to the Trojans at the same Coliseum.

Few entries in the Notre Dame record book have a gap as sizable as the one that separates the No. 1 figure for individual passing yardage in one game and the runner-up mark. And that's remarkable, considering the Fighting Irish have boasted a wealth of talent at quarterback— including four Heisman Trophy winners—dating to the days of Gus Dorais. It seems logical there would be a logjam at the top of virtually every passing category, but Joe Theismann would have none of that. On November 28, 1970, Theismann obliterated the Fighting Irish record for passing yards in one game—Terry Hanratty had established the mark with 366 against Purdue in 1967—when he threw for 526 yards against Southern California on a rainy day at the Los Angeles Memorial Coliseum. That was the good news; the bad news was that Notre Dame, unbeaten and untied entering the game, lost to the Trojans, 38-28, and saw its national-championship hopes dashed. Theismann completed a school-record 33 passes in 58 attempts and threw for two touchdowns, hitting John Cieszkowski on a nine-yard play and connecting with Larry Parker on a 46-yard strike. He also had 25- and one-yard scor-

Despite a school-record passing effort by quarterback Joe Theismann, Notre Dame still managed to drop a 38-28 decision to Southern Cal in 1970.

NOTRE DAME STADIUM

Fighting Irish, wearing special green jerseys and emotionally charged, pound USC 49-19 en route to national championship, Oct. 22, 1977

Spanking new Notre Dame Stadium opens with 20-14 Fighting Irish win over SMU, Oct. 4, 1930

Heisman hopeful Tim Brown gains momentum with TD punt returns of 71 and 66 yards in home-opening 31-8 win over Michigan State, Sept. 19, 1987

Home of nine championship teams and seven Heisman Trophy winners— (left to right) Johnny Lujack (1947), Angelo Bertelli (1943), Leon Hart (1949), Tim Brown (1987), Paul Hornung (1956), John Huarte (1964), John Lattner (1953)

Safety Pat Terrell knocks away Steve Walsh's two-point conversion pass with 45 seconds remaining to preserve 31-30 upset of No. 1-ranked Miami, Oct. 15, 1988

Highlight of 35-3 victory over Georgia Tech is 96-yard TD pass from Blair Kiel to Joe Howard, Nov. 7, 1981

'House that Rockne Built' also became stomping grounds for championship coaches Frank Leahy, Ara Parseghian, Dan Devine and Lou Holtz

Harry Oliver's 51-yard field goal with no time remaining stuns Michigan, 29-27, Sept. 20, 1980

Where last-second passes by Florida State QB Charlie Ward were batted down by Thomas Knight and Shawn Wooden, preserving 31-24 win over top-ranked Seminoles, Nov. 13, 1993

Raghib Ismail does his best "rocket" impersonation, returning kickoffs 87 and 83 yards for touchdowns in 54-11 win over Rice, Nov. 5, 1988

1966 championship season opens in record fashion for receiver Jim Seymour—13 catches for 276 yards, 3 TDs in win over Purdue

NOTRE DAME STADIUM

(1930 -)

It has stood for almost three-quarters of a century, Knute Rockne's gift to the proud football future he choreographed but could not share. No college sports facility has served as home to more national championship teams, Heisman Trophy winners, consensus All-Americans, memorable moments and legendary players than Notre Dame Stadium, where Rockne christened his vision in 1930 with a 10-0 record.

That was the first of the Stadium's nine title teams and the last coaching season for Rockne, who died in a 1931 plane crash. But the Rockne aura, the incredible championship mystique, still wafts through the

Where USC's Johnny Baker connected on 23-yard field goal with 1 minute remaining to end Notre Dame's 26-game unbeaten streak, Nov. 21, 1931

QB John Huarte, setting tone for Heisman Trophy-winning 1964 season, fires two TD passes in home opener, a 34-15 win over Purdue

Highlight of Nov. 11, 1989, rout of SMU is Ricky Watters' school-record 97-yard TD punt return

In 1993 regular-season finale, David Gordon crushes Irish championship hopes with final-play 41-yard field goal that gives Boston College 41-39 win

Great Notre Dame passing combos: Huarte-to-Snow, Hanratty-to-Seymour, Theismann-to-Gatewood, Clements-to-Demmerle, Montana-to-MacAfee, Beuerlein (right)-to-Brown

Where Frank Varrichione and other Fighting Irish players resorted to "fainting tactics" to gain 14-14 tie against Iowa, Nov. 21, 1953

Rick Mirer's three-yard TD pass to Jerome Bettis and two-point conversion pass to Reggie Brooks with 20 seconds remaining give Irish 17-16 win over Penn State in 1992 "Snow Game."

Fighting Irish defeat Michigan, 23-17, in raucous 1982 season opener—and first night game at Notre Dame Stadium

Where Craig Hentrich kicked school-record five field goals in 29-20 win over No. 2-ranked Miami, Oct. 20, 1990

Season-opening win over North Carolina stretches four-year unbeaten streak to 39, Sept. 30, 1950

Two-time defending-champion Irish extend winning streak to 21 with 46-0 victory over Washington, Nov. 27, 1948

single-decked, oval football structure and feeds the frenzy of the game's most passionate, tradition-minded and celebrated fans. Notre Dame Stadium is no ordinary house of worship—it's a shrine, matched in renown only by a select few sports venues in the world.

The $750,000 structure, patterned on a smaller scale after massive Michigan Stadium, was a necessary replacement for Cartier Field, a no-frills turn-of-the-century facility that could shoehorn 30,000 fans through its rickety gates for special games. The incredible success of Rockne's football program and his vision for a victory-filled future dictated the need

for a new stadium and the coach had a hand in every phase of its construction, from design and location to parking and traffic systems.

That Rockne's final Notre Dame team won a national championship in his only season at the Stadium was fitting—and eerily ironic. Though future championships would be produced by such coaches as Frank Leahy (4), Ara Parseghian (2), Dan Devine (1) and Lou Holtz (1), the Rockne influence has never been lost.

Notre Dame Stadium, located just south of the for-mer Cartier Field site on the southeast edge of a tightly knit campus, was surrounded for many years

Oval, single-decked Notre Dame Stadium, renovated and expanded before the 1997 season, has stood for more than seven decades.

by a red-brick outer wall. But the inside colors of choice were blue, gold and green, worn by players, students, alumni and local fans who cheered seven Heisman winners, 83 consensus All-Americans and teams that almost routinely contended for national honors while playing some of the toughest schedules in the nation.

Early capacity of Notre Dame Stadium was 50,000-54,000; from 1966 through 1996, it was listed as 59,075. Every game but one (Thanksgiving Day, 1973) over that 31-season span was a sellout, a streak that continues today after the addition of 21,000 seats in a $50 million expansion and renovation. Entering the 2003 campaign, with a capacity now listed at 80,795, the Notre Dame sellout streak stood at 173—and an amazing 215 in 216 games.

The expansion, which was completed before the 1997 campaign, was more cosmetic than intrusive.

Today's fans still enjoy near-perfect sight lines and a sense of being close to the action, a result of the stadium's oval shape and single-deck design. Notre Dame officials took care not to sacrifice tradition for modern conveniences.

A yellow-brick facade now encloses the red-brick outer wall of yesteryear, giving longtime fans a weekly shot of deja vu. Fans in the south end zone stands can still see the 132-foot high "Touchdown Jesus" mural rising above the north end zone seats on the side of 14-story Hesburgh Library, players in the expanded locker rooms are surrounded by salvaged brick from the old complex and games are played on a new natural grass field. Two new scoreboards, a three-tier press box and park-like landscaping around the stadium add to the atmosphere, as does the absence of three rows of the permanent stands that were *removed* because of bad sight lines.

Fans in the south end zone stands at crowded Notre Dame Stadium can see 14-story Hesburgh Library and its giant 'Touchdown Jesus' mural rising over the opposite end zone.

Here are a few landmark moments and historical notes about Notre Dame Stadium:

■ **First game:** October 4, 1930. The Fighting Irish gave coach Knute Rockne a 20-14 victory over SMU in the Stadium debut, the first of 10 straight wins in a championship season.

■ **Dedication game:** October 11, 1930. More than 40,000 fans watched the fired-up Fighting Irish defeat traditional rival Navy, 26-2.

■ **First night game:** September 18, 1982. A rousing 23-17 win over Michigan punctuated the first game under lights in the opener of the Stadium's 53rd season.

■ **300th game at the Stadium:** November 9, 1991. Tennessee scored a touchdown with 4:03 remaining to beat the Fighting Irish, 35-34.

■ **1,000th game in Notre Dame history:** September 5, 1996. A landmark contest ended on a happy note as the Fighting Irish beat Vanderbilt, 14-7.

■ **Rededication game:** September 6, 1997. Georgia Tech fell, 17-13, in the first game at expanded and renovated Notre Dame Stadium.

■ **Championship teams:** 1930, '43, '46, '47, '49, '66, '73, '77, '88.

■ **Heisman Trophy winners:** Angelo Bertelli, 1943; Johnny Lujack, 1947; Leon Hart, 1949; John Lattner, 1953; Paul Hornung, 1956; John Huarte, 1964; Tim Brown, 1987.

CHRONOLOGY

1887

Won-lost-tied record: 0-1-0

Notre Dame plays its first football game on November 23. It loses to Michigan, 8-0, in South Bend.

DID YOU KNOW ... THAT THE FIRST TOUCHDOWN IN NOTRE DAME HISTORY—SCORED ON A RUN BY HARRY JEWETT AGAINST MICHIGAN IN 1888—COVERED FIVE YARDS?

Notre Dame plays the formative years of its football program on an open field. (In the late 1890s, Warren Cartier, an 1887 Notre Dame graduate, supplies the building materials for an enclosed field and grandstand, a facility that evolves into what is known as Cartier Field.)

1888

1-2-0

Harry Jewett scores the first touchdown in Notre Dame history on April 20 against Michigan. Notre Dame loses that game, 26-6, and falls to the Wolverines, 10-4, the next day in another out-of-season matchup.

Touchdowns are worth four points in football's early years.

Notre Dame defeats Harvard School of Chicago ("Harvard Prep"), 20-0, on December 6 for its first football triumph.

1889

1-0-0

Notre Dame defeats Northwestern, 9-0.

1890-1891

No football program.

1892

1-0-1

Notre Dame overwhelms South Bend High School, 56-0, but is played to a 10-10 tie by Hillsdale College.

1893

4-1-0

Notre Dame wins its first four games, then loses to the University of Chicago, 8-0.

1894

3-1-1

James L. Morrison becomes the first official football coach at Notre Dame.

Albion College accounts for the two blemishes on Notre Dame's record, earning a 6-6 tie and then posting a 19-12 victory in a rematch.

1895

3-1-0

H.G. Hadden takes over as Irish coach. Notre Dame's lone loss is to Indianapolis Artillery, 18-0.

1896

4-3-0

Under new coach **Frank E. Hering**, Notre Dame plays Purdue for the first time and loses to the Boilermakers, 28-22.

1897

4-1-1

Notre Dame shuts out four opponents, although one of them, Rush Medical, manages a scoreless tie.

Mike Daly kicks the first field goal in school history, a 35-yarder, against Chicago.

1898

4-2-0

A beefed-up schedule includes games with Illinois, Michigan State, Michigan and Indiana. Notre Dame splits those four games and defeats DePauw and Albion.

Touchdowns now count five points.

1899

6-3-1

Notre Dame plays its first 10-game schedule.

Some researchers date the use of the "Fighting Irish" nickname to this season.

The second-ever meeting with Purdue ends in a 10-10 deadlock.

James McWeeney is the Notre Dame coach.

1900

6-3-1

1900 FIGHTING IRISH

Notre Dame, with Pat O'Dea serving as coach, wins its first four games by a combined score of 245-0 but manages only 16 points in its last six games.

The first meeting with Wisconsin is a disaster as the Badgers win, 54-0, in Madison.

1901

8-1-1

Only three of Notre Dame's opponents are big-name schools.

The opposition scores only 19 points in 10 games.

The Fighting Irish defeat Purdue for the first time, winning by a 12-6 score.

1902

6-2-1

1902 FIGHTING IRISH

James F. Faragher, a member of the 1900 and 1901 Notre Dame teams, is listed as coach but captain Louis "Red" Salmon, a junior, also receives credit for running the team in this era of part-time coaches.

In a sparkling season opener, the Fighting Irish rout Michigan State, 33-0.

Michigan and Knox College deal Notre Dame its losses, and Purdue plays the Irish to a 6-6 tie in the season finale.

1903

8-0-1

The Irish take advantage of a schedule that includes four medical schools and only two major universities, shutting out all nine of its opponents.

Against quality opposition, Notre

Dame downs Michigan State, 12-0, and battles Northwestern to a scoreless deadlock.

1904

5-3-0

After seeing coaching duty as a player in the previous two seasons, Salmon now serves in an official coach-only capacity.

The Irish play their first game west of the Mississippi, losing at Kansas, 24-5. Frank Shaughnessy returns a fumble 107 yards for a touchdown against the Jayhawks. (The playing field is 110 yards long.)

1905

5-4-0

Another former Notre Dame player, Henry "Fuzzy" McGlew, oversees the team in place of Salmon.

After being shut out in consecutive games by Wisconsin and Wabash College, the Fighting Irish annihilate American Medical, 142-0, in a

game shortened to only 33 minutes.

Bill Downs scores six touchdowns against DePauw.

1906

6-1-0

Thomas A. Barry, a former star player at Brown, is named coach.

The Fighting Irish shut out six opponents—Michigan State and Purdue are among the victims— but lose to Indiana, 12-0, in a game played in Indianapolis.

1907

6-0-1

Indiana again spoils Notre Dame's bid for a perfect season. This time, the Hoosiers tie the Fighting Irish, 0-0.

1908

8-1-0

In Victor M. Place's only season as coach, the Fighting Irish stumble only once—in Week 3, when they suffer a 12-6 loss at Michigan.

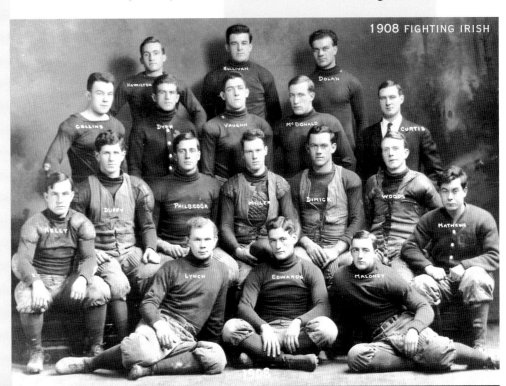

1908 FIGHTING IRISH

DID YOU KNOW ... THAT THE FIGHTING IRISH LED, 111-0, AT HALFTIME OF THEIR 1905 GAME AGAINST AMERICAN MEDICAL?

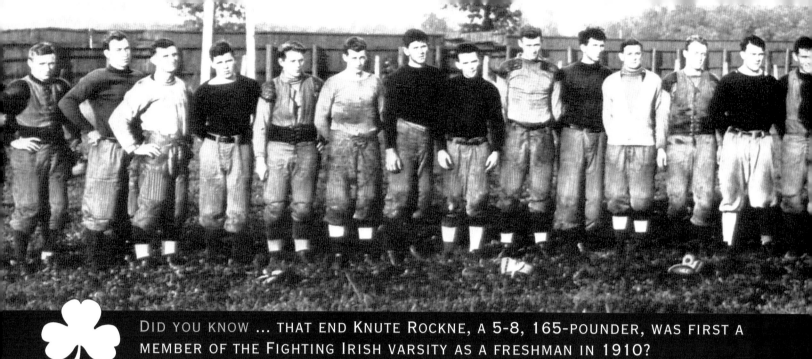

1909

7-0-1

1909 FIGHTING IRISH

The "Notre Dame Victory March" is first performed on campus.

Notre Dame wins national acclaim with an 11-3 victory over powerful Michigan in Ann Arbor. The win comes in the first of Frank "Shorty" Longman's two seasons as Fighting Irish coach.

Harry "Red" Miller returns a punt 95 yards against Olivet but fails to score.

The Irish are unbeaten and untied through seven games, outscoring opponents, 236-14, but hopes for a perfect season die in a season-ending 0-0 tie at Marquette.

1910

4-1-1

Finding it difficult to schedule marquee teams as it becomes a force in college football, Notre Dame plays four small schools and two with national stature. The Irish outscore the undermanned competition, 187-3, but lose to Michigan State (17-0) and tie Marquette (5-5).

1911

6-0-2

Art Smith runs for a school-record seven touchdowns against Loyola of Chicago in Notre Dame's 80-0 triumph.

Alfred Bergman returns a kickoff 105 yards against Loyola but does not score.

The Fighting Irish, now coached by John L. Marks, again maul inferior opponents—this time by a cumulative 222-9 score over six games—but are held to 0-0 ties against major-college foes Pittsburgh and Marquette.

1912

7-0-0

Notre Dame completes its first perfect season (minimum of five games). The schedule includes lightweights St.

Viator, Adrian College, Morris Harvey and Wabash, but the Irish also take the measure of Pittsburgh (3-0), Saint Louis (47-7) and Marquette (69-0).

Touchdowns are now six points.

The playing field is reduced from 110 yards to 100, with two 10-yard end zones.

1913

7-0-0

Jesse Harper arrives as football coach and athletic director.

1912 FIGHTING IRISH

The schedule gets an immediate upgrade, with Notre Dame to meet Army, Penn State and Texas for the first time.

In a November 1 game at West Point, quarterback Gus Dorais

and end Knute Rockne demonstrate to the nation just how devastating a passing game can be. Their exploits help the Fighting Irish blitz Army, 35-13, and boost Notre Dame's reputation as an emerging big-time power.

The Irish win at Penn State, 14-7, and at Texas, 30-7, the latter victory capping a perfect season.

Dorais is Notre Dame's first consensus All-American.

The Fighting Irish's record from 1906 through 1913 is 51-3-5.

1914

6-2-0

Venturing to the East takes its toll this time as Notre Dame falls at Yale, 28-0, and at Army, 20-7.

1915

7-1-0

Harper's Irish finish the season with four consecutive victories on the road but hopes for a perfect season had ended earlier with a 20-19 loss at Nebraska.

1916

8-1-0

Notre Dame wins its first four games by a 182-0 score and its

last four by a 101-0 count. But on November 4, the Fighting Irish absorb a 30-10 drubbing at Army.

Chet Grant returns a punt 95 yards for a score against Case Tech.

1917

6-1-1

Center Frank Rydzewski is a consensus All-American.

After starting 1-1-1, Notre Dame wins its final five games—a run that includes wins over Army and Michigan State.

Harper resigns after the season. His record over five years is 34-5-1.

1918

3-1-2

The Knute Rockne coaching era begins. Rockne, who was a starter at end for the Fighting Irish from 1911 through 1913 and then was an assistant coach under Harper, achieves victory No. 1 in Notre Dame's season-opening 26-6 triumph over Case Tech.

Rockne tastes defeat for the first

time in Week 4 as Michigan State edges the Irish, 13-7.

Curly Lambeau, who would become founder and longtime coach (six NFL titles) of the Green Bay Packers, is the No. 1 fullback on Rockne's first Irish team.

1919

9-0-0

Rockne's team runs the table, although Nebraska, a 14-9 loser, and Army, which comes within 12-9, offer stiff tests.

> **DID YOU KNOW … THAT GEORGE GIPP RETURNED EIGHT KICKOFFS AND TWO PUNTS FOR A TOTAL OF 207 YARDS IN A 1920 GAME AGAINST ARMY?**

Halfback George Gipp averages 6.9 yards per carry, scores seven touchdowns and passes for three TDs.

1920

9-0-0

Gipp is a consensus All-American in Notre Dame's perfect season after averaging 8.1 yards per rushing attempt, making eight TDs and throwing for three scores.

Gipp sits out most of the Northwestern game because of a

shoulder injury and misses the final game of the season, against Michigan State, because of a strep throat.

Gipp, 25, dies of complications from the throat infection on December 14.

End **Eddie Anderson** has three TD receptions against Northwestern.

1921
10-1-0

Anderson is a consensus All-American. He finishes with 26 receptions, a figure that will stand as the school record for nearly three decades.

John Mohardt throws nine touchdown passes, runs for 781 yards and scores 12 touchdowns.

Iowa deals Notre Dame its lone loss with a 10-7 victory in Week 3.

1922
8-1-1

South Bend's WSBT is the first radio station to carry a Notre Dame game. It covers the November 4 Homecoming game against Indiana. The Irish win, 27-0.

Paul Castner sets a still-standing Irish record for kickoff-return yards in one game, totaling 253 in the season opener against Kalamazoo. He scores twice on returns against the Michigan school, once going 95 yards.

Over the season, Castner returns 11 kickoffs for 490 yards, a Notre Dame record average of 44.5.

Unbeaten through Week 6, the Irish then tie Army, 0-0, and lose at Nebraska, 14-6, three weeks later.

1923
9-1-0

For the second consecutive season, Nebraska deals Notre Dame its only loss. This time, the Cornhuskers win, 14-7.

Successive victories over Army, Princeton, Georgia Tech and Purdue highlight the season.

Don Miller averages 7.8 yards per carry. Miller and fellow halfback Red Maher each score 10 touchdowns.

1924
10-0-0

The Irish are national champions for the first time.

Quarterback **Harry Stuhldreher**, halfback Jim Crowley and fullback Elmer Layden of Four Horsemen fame are consensus All-Americans.

DID YOU KNOW ... THAT CARNEGIE TECH WON FOUR TIMES IN 19 MEETINGS WITH THE IRISH?

The Horsemen are so dominant in a game against Army in New York that sportswriter Grantland Rice pens his memorable "Outlined against a blue-gray October sky" description of the Notre Dame stars.

The backs operate behind the formidable Seven Mules line.

Miller leads the team in rushing with 763 yards.

After victories over outmanned Lombard and Wabash, the Fighting Irish defeat Army, Princeton, Georgia Tech, Wisconsin,

Nebraska, Northwestern and Carnegie Tech.

In the Rose Bowl, the Irish capitalize on Stanford mistakes and stop Pop Warner's team, 27-10.

1925
7-2-1

Notre Dame is held scoreless three times as Rockne suffers his first two-loss season.

Leading passer Harry O'Boyle throws for only 107 yards and the ground game, led by Christy Flanagan's 556 yards, is not overwhelming. Yet

STUHLDREHER

Rockne coaxes seven victories and a 0-0 tie with Penn State out of this group.

DID YOU KNOW ... THAT NOTRE DAME WAS UNBEATEN AT HOME IN 93 CONSECUTIVE GAMES (90-0-3 RECORD) FROM THE MIDPOINT OF THE 1905 SEASON TO LATE IN THE 1928 SEASON?

Nebraska scores its third victory over a Rockne-coached Notre Dame team. (No other opponent defeats Rockne that many times.)

1926
9-1-0

Center Bud Boeringer is a consensus All-American.

The Irish reel off eight victories before getting stuffed by Carnegie Tech, 19-0.

Notre Dame and Southern California clash for the first time in the season finale and the Irish come away with a 13-12 victory in Los Angeles.

1927
7-1-1

"Fighting Irish" is officially adopted as Notre Dame's nickname. The term has been used for years, though.

The Irish play before their first crowd of 100,000—the count actually is 120,000—and edge Southern California, 7-6, at Soldier Field in Chicago.

Notre Dame plays Navy for the first time and defeats the Midshipmen, 19-6, in Baltimore.

Guard John Smith, Notre Dame's captain, is a consensus All-American.

1928
5-4-0

The Fighting Irish play their final season at Cartier Field.

Notre Dame loses four games for only the second time in its history.

The Irish suffer their first home defeat since 1905, falling to Carnegie Tech, 27-7, on November 17. The setback comes one week after Notre Dame's "win one for the Gipper" triumph against Army.

Southern California notches its first victory over the Irish, 27-14. The Carnegie Tech and USC defeats are Notre Dame's only back-to-back losses under Rockne.

1929
9-0

With excavation work in progress for a new stadium, Notre Dame is forced to play all nine of its games on the road. Yet the Irish go undefeated and untied and are declared national champions. They play three games at Chicago's Soldier Field, which is relatively close to home.

Quarterback Frank Carideo and guard Jack Cannon are consensus All-Americans.

Notre Dame scores 14 or fewer points five times but the defense comes up big.

Rockne, suffering from phlebitis, is not his usual constant presence on the sidelines.

1930
10-0

The Irish are national champs.

Carideo and halfback Marchy Schwartz are consensus All-Americans.

Notre Dame Stadium opens on October 4. Southern Methodist proves to be a pesky foe in the first game, but the Fighting Irish prevail, 20-14. Joe Savoldi sparks the victory with a 100-yard kickoff return.

The stadium is dedicated on October 11. Notre Dame makes it a festive occasion by routing Navy, 26-2.

The Irish cap the season by

1929 FIGHTING IRISH

thumping Southern California, 27-0, in Los Angeles.

Schwartz rushes for 927 yards, a Notre Dame season high.

1931
6-2-1

On March 31, Rockne dies in an airplane crash in Kansas.

Heartley "Hunk" Anderson, who played under Rockne at Notre Dame and was an Irish assistant coach in 1930, is named coach.

Anderson's team is undefeated and once-tied through seven games but ends the season with losses to Southern California and Army.

The first capacity crowd at Notre Dame Stadium, a throng of 50,731, is on hand for the USC game. The Trojans win, 16-14, on John Baker's field goal with one minute to play and snap Notre Dame's unbeaten streak at 26 games.

Schwartz and center Tommy Yarr are consensus All-Americans.

Lew Ayres stars in the motion picture "The Spirit of Notre Dame."

1932
7-2-0

Tackle Joe Kurth is a consensus All-American.

Only three teams manage to score against Notre Dame, but two of them wind up with victories. Pittsburgh prevails, 12-0, and Southern California wins, 13-0.

George Melinkovich returns a Northwestern kickoff 98 yards for a touchdown.

1933
3-5-1

End **Hugh Devore**, a future Notre Dame coach, is co-captain of the Fighting Irish.

After a season-opening tie against Kansas and a win against Indiana, Notre Dame loses four in a row (all are shutouts) for the first time in its history. Coach Anderson comes under heavy fire.

The Fighting Irish win two of their last three games, but not even a thrilling victory over Army in the season finale can save Anderson's job.

Tackle Ed "Moose" Krause, who would serve as Notre Dame athletic director from 1949 through 1981, winds up a three-year football career with the Irish.

1934
6-3-0

Elmer Layden, a member of the Fighting Irish's fabled Four Horsemen a decade earlier, leaves as coach at Duquesne to replace Anderson at Notre Dame.

Layden gets off on the wrong foot as the Irish drop their season opener, 7-6, to Texas, but Notre Dame wins six of its final eight games.

Layden's stock rises when the Irish end the season with victories over Army and Southern California.

Center Jack Robinson is a consensus All-American.

DID YOU KNOW ... THAT THE IRISH FAILED TO SCORE IN SIX OF THEIR NINE GAMES IN 1933?

1935

7-1-1

Tackle and captain-elect Joe Sullivan dies of pneumonia in March.

Bill Shakespeare gets off an Irish-record 86-yard punt against Pittsburgh.

1936

6-2-1

The Associated Press releases its first-ever college football poll on October 19. Sportswriters and broadcasters handle the voting. Minnesota tops the initial rankings and Notre Dame is No. 7.

1939

7-2-0

The Fighting Irish conquer rivals Purdue and Army but fall to Southern California.

End Wayne Millner, a consensus All-American, hauls in a touchdown pass from Shakespeare in the final half-minute as Notre Dame rallies for an 18-13 victory at Ohio State in a much-hyped battle of unbeaten teams. Irish scrub quarterback Jim McKenna, who had sneaked aboard the train to Columbus and hoped to find a seat in the stands, winds up dressing for the game and brings in the winning play in a messenger role.

After the dramatic win over the Buckeyes, Notre Dame loses to Northwestern and is tied by Army before completing the season with a 20-13 triumph over Southern California.

SHAKESPEARE

In the final AP poll of the season, the Gophers are No. 1 and the Fighting Irish are eighth.

1937

6-2-1

Notre Dame manages a mere 77 points in its nine games and scores nine or fewer points in seven consecutive games. Still, the Irish win six times—Army and Southern California are among their victims—and tie Illinois.

End Chuck Sweeney is a consensus All-American.

1938

8-1-0

Notre Dame reaches the top of the AP poll for the first time on November 14. The Fighting Irish are No. 1 the next two weeks as well but drop from first to fifth after losing to Southern California, 13-0.

Tackle Ed Beinor is a consensus All-American.

1940

7-2-0

Notre Dame wins its first six games, one of them a 61-0 crushing of Carnegie Tech, a pesky opponent over the years.

The Irish are dealt consecutive defeats for the first time since 1934 when Iowa and then Northwestern score victories.

The motion picture "Knute Rockne, All American" makes its debut. Pat O'Brien is cast as Rockne and Ronald Reagan as George Gipp.

1941

8-0-1

Layden resigns as coach in February to become commissioner of the National Football League. His successor is former Notre Dame player **Frank Leahy**, who had compiled a 20-2 record in two seasons at Boston College.

Leahy's first Irish team, paced by sophomore Angelo Bertelli's eight touchdown passes, misses a

DID YOU KNOW ... THAT WHEN ANGELO BERTELLI BECAME NOTRE DAME'S FIRST HEISMAN TROPHY WINNER IN 1943, TEAMMATE CREIGHTON MILLER FINISHED FOURTH IN THE VOTING?

perfect season when Army plays it to a scoreless tie in Week 6.

End Bob Dove is a consensus All-American.

1942

7-2-2

Leahy incurs his first loss as Notre Dame coach when Georgia Tech edges the Fighting Irish, 13-6, in Week 2. The defeat comes after the Irish play Wisconsin to a 7-7 tie.

Bertelli throws four touchdown passes against Stanford (a feat equaled but never surpassed in Notre Dame history) and finishes the season with 10 TD strikes.

Dove repeats as a consensus All-American.

1943

9-1-0

Leahy's Irish are national champions. They lead every AP poll of the season, and not even a season-ending loss to Great Lakes Naval Training Station can budge Notre Dame from the top spot.

Quarterback **Bertelli** wins the Heisman Trophy despite playing in only six games before entering military service.

Bertelli, halfback Creighton Miller, guard Pat Filley, tackle Jim White and end John Yonakor give Notre Dame a school-record five consensus All-Americans.

Miller runs for 911 yards, the top figure in the country. (Entering 2003, Miller remains the only Notre Dame player to lead the nation in rushing since the NCAA began releasing official statistics in 1937.)

BERTELLI

1944

8-2-0

With Leahy serving in the U.S. Navy, assistant coach Ed McKeever takes over as coach.

Quarterback Johnny Lujack, who stood out as Bertelli's fill-in late in the 1943 season, is among the many college players nationwide serving military duty.

Frank Dancewicz takes over at quarterback.

The season is a good one in terms of the won-lost record, but Notre Dame's two defeats sting. Having beaten Navy seven consecutive times, the Irish are walloped, 32-13, by the Midshipmen in a game played at Baltimore, Then, the next week, Army buries Notre Dame, 59-0, at Yankee Stadium. Dancewicz,

who has a creditable season with nine touchdown passes, is intercepted seven times by the Cadets.

The Irish finish ninth in the AP poll.

1945

7-2-1

McKeever becomes coach at Cornell. **Hugh Devore**, a Notre  Dame assistant, replaces McKeever.

The Fighting Irish take a perfect record into Week 6 but are tied by Navy. The next week, they play Army at Yankee Stadium for the 15th consecutive year. Hoping to atone for the embarrassing loss of 1944, the Irish suffer a near repeat as the Cadets coast, 48-0.

Great Lakes also defeats Notre Dame, which again winds up No. 9 in the AP rankings.

1946

8-0-1

Leahy returns from the Navy and coaches the Irish to the national championship.

In a storied struggle between No. 1 Army and No. 2 Notre Dame on November 9 at Yankee Stadium, the teams battle to a 0-0 tie.

In Notre Dame's eight other games, no team comes closer than 20 points to the Irish.

Notre Dame's strong finish to the season and Army's narrow win over a subpar Navy team sway AP poll voters, who elevate the Irish to the No. 1 slot.

Lujack, back from the service, and tackle George Connor are consensus All-Americans.

The first-ever Outland Trophy, honoring the nation's best interior lineman, goes to Connor.

Notre Dame opponents score a total of 24 points.

1947

9-0-0

LIVINGSTONE

within two touchdowns.

The Irish wallop Army, 27-7, at South Bend in the last meeting of the powerhouse teams for a decade. The schools decide that the rivalry has grown too big and needs a cooling-off period.

Lujack wins the Heisman Trophy. He completes 56 percent of his passes and throws for nine touchdowns.

Halfback **Bob Livingstone** sets a still-existing Irish record for the longest run from scrimmage, going 92 yards for a touchdown against Southern California.

1948

9-0-1

Fischer, end Leon Hart and halfback Emil Sitko are consensus All-Americans.

Fischer wins the Outland Trophy.

Notre Dame is No. 1 in the AP poll in early October and again in early November, but unbeaten and untied Michigan is atop the rankings at season's end.

The lone blemish on the No. 2 Fighting Irish's record is a 14-14 tie at Southern California in the season finale.

FISCHER

DID YOU KNOW ... THAT FUTURE PRO GEORGE RATTERMAN WAS NOTRE DAME'S NO. 2 QUARTERBACK IN 1945 AND 1946?

The Fighting Irish repeat as national champs.

Northwestern gives Notre Dame a tough game in Week 7 but loses, 26-19. None of the Irish's eight other opponents come

Lujack, Connor and guard **Bill Fischer** are consensus All-Americans.

Halfback Terry Brennan scores 11 TDs.

LATTNER

1949

10-0-0

Leahy's Irish are national champs and push their amazing unbeaten streak to 38 games (36-0-2).

Hart, who makes five TD receptions, wins the Heisman Trophy.

Notre Dame, which scores 27 or more points in every game, is particularly impressive in a 46-7 dismantling of No. 4-ranked Tulane and a 32-0 trouncing of rival Southern California.

Quarterback Bob Williams sets school records with 16 touchdown passes and 1,374 yards passing.

Halfback **Larry Coutre** goes 91 yards for a TD against Navy.

Hart, Sitko and Williams are consensus All-Americans.

1950

4-4-1

The Fighting Irish win their opener against North Carolina but are jolted by Purdue, 28-14, in Week 2. The Boilermakers' triumph ends Notre Dame's 39-game undefeated streak that dates to 1946 and its 28-game home winning streak that goes back to 1942.

The Irish experience their first non-winning season since 1933.

John Petitbon averages 17.1 yards on 10 carries against Michigan State.

End Jim Mutscheller and center Jerry Groom are standouts. Mutscheller sets Notre Dame records with 35 receptions, 426 receiving yards and seven TD catches. Groom is a consensus All-American.

The United Press begins its college football poll, with coaches doing the voting.

1951

7-2-1

Notre Dame plays its first night game, defeating the University of Detroit, 40-6, at Briggs Stadium in Detroit.

The Irish suffer their worst-ever loss under Leahy, a 35-0 thumping by Michigan State.

1952

7-2-1

Halfback **Johnny Lattner** rushes for 732 yards and is a consensus All-American.

Fullback Neil Worden scores 10 touchdowns.

After a 1-1-1 start, Notre Dame wins six of its final seven games—including a 27-21 triumph over Oklahoma in the first meeting of two of college football's marquee teams.

AP and UP both rank the Irish third at season's end.

DID YOU KNOW ... THAT BRONKO NAGURSKI JR. WAS A STARTING TACKLE FOR TERRY BRENNAN'S 1956 AND 1957 NOTRE DAME TEAMS?

1953

9-0-1

Lattner, an outstanding runner, defender, punter and return man, wins the Heisman Trophy. He is the fourth Notre Dame player to win the award under Leahy.

Lattner and tackle Art Hunter are consensus All-Americans.

The Fighting Irish finish second to Maryland in both wire-service polls.

Leahy and Notre Dame are criticized for their tactics in salvaging a late-season 14-14 tie with Iowa. The Irish apparently fake injuries in the late stages of each half, the timeouts giving Notre Dame enough time to score touchdowns.

Joe Heap gets the Fighting Irish off and running against Southern California with a 94-yard punt return for a TD. The Irish roll to a 48-14 victory.

Worden runs for 859 yards and scores 11 TDs.

Tackle Wayne Edmonds and halfback Dick Washington are the first black players in Notre Dame history.

Leahy suffers from pancreatitis and other health problems during the season.

1954

9-1-0

In late January, Leahy resigns as Notre Dame coach. He cites health reasons.

Leahy's successor is former Notre Dame star **Terry Brennan**, who served as Irish freshmen coach in 1953 and is only two years removed from

coaching in the Chicago high school ranks.

Brennan turns 26 in June.

The Brennan era begins with a 21-0 triumph over Texas.

The Irish are defeated by Purdue in Week 2 but don't lose the rest of the way.

Halfback Heap rambles 89 yards for a touchdown in a season-ending 26-14 win over SMU.

The Irish are ranked No. 4 in both final polls.

Quarterback **Ralph Guglielmi** is

a consensus All-American.

1955

8-2-0

Quarterback Paul Hornung is a consensus All-American. He passes for 743 yards and nine touchdowns for a Notre Dame team that is ranked ninth at season's end by AP and 10th by UP.

Hornung and halfback Jim Morse hook up on a 78-yard TD pass in the season finale against Southern California, but the Trojans break open a tight game and win, 42-20. Morse finishes the day with five receptions for 208 yards, a 41.6 average.

1956

2-8-0

Hornung throws for 917 yards, rushes for a team-high 420 yards and wins the Heisman Trophy.

Hornung fails to win consensus All-American honors at his position. That honor goes to Stanford's John Brodie.

It's a dismal season overall under the Golden Dome. Ranked No. 3 in the preseason AP poll, the Irish defeat only Indiana and North Carolina. They lose five in a row in a stretch that includes a 47-14 loss to No. 2 Michigan State, a 40-0 pounding at the hands of top-ranked Oklahoma and a 33-7 pasting by Navy.

1957

7-3-0

Notre Dame and Army clash for the first time in 10 years. Sophomore **Monty Stickles**' 39-yard field goal enables the Fighting Irish to squeak by the Cadets, 23-21, in a stemwinder

STICKLES

at Philadelphia.

After losing consecutive games to Navy and Michigan State on the heels of a 4-0 start, the Irish shock the college football world by ending Oklahoma's record 47-game winning streak. Notre Dame wins, 7-0, in Norman, Okla.

Notre Dame had been the last team to defeat Oklahoma, winning by a 28-21 score in the 1953 season opener.

Guard Al Ecuyer is a consensus All-American.

1958

6-4-0

George Izo's nine touchdown passes and

Stickles' seven TD receptions fuel the offense.

After starting the season with victories over Indiana and SMU, the Irish fall into a lose-one, win-one pattern over the final eight weeks.

Brennan's five-year record of 32-18 (.640

IZO

winning percentage) is impressive by most standards— but not by those at Notre Dame. Brennan is fired, and the dismissal—considered unfair in most quarters—is met with an outcry nationwide.

1959

5-5-0

Joe Kuharich, who had coached the Washington Redskins the previous five years and played under Elmer Layden at Notre Dame, takes over as Irish coach.

Notre Dame loses four of five games in one span.

Season-ending victories over Iowa and Southern California avert a losing season.

End Stickles is a consensus All-American.

1960

2-8-0

Notre Dame opens with a 21-7 triumph over California but then endures a school-record eight consecutive defeats.

A 17-0 win over Southern California in the season finale provides some consolation.

The Fighting Irish's No. 1 passer, George Haffner, completes only 30 of 108 attempts and leading rusher Angelo Dabiero gains only 325 yards.

1961

5-5-0

The Irish start the season impressively with wins over

LAMONICA

Oklahoma, Purdue and Southern California but drop five of their final seven games.

The season ends with a thud in 42-21 and 37-13 losses to Iowa and Duke, respectively.

Dabiero rushes for 6.9 yards per carry in a 637-yard season.

1962

5-5-0

A victory in the season finale against top-ranked Southern California would give Kuharich his first winning season as Notre Dame coach, but the Irish are no match for the Trojans, who prevail, 25-0.

Daryle Lamonica tosses four touchdown passes against Pittsburgh.

The season is the last for Kuharich, who becomes the only coach in Notre Dame history to finish with a career losing record. His mark: 17-23.

1963

2-7-0

Hugh Devore, who had coached the Irish in 1945 and guided the freshmen team in the Kuharich years, is back as Notre Dame coach. He had been coach of the NFL's Philadelphia Eagles in 1956 and 1957.

The Irish defeat Southern California and UCLA on successive weekends in October for their only victories of the year.

The Notre Dame-Iowa game, scheduled for November 23, is canceled after President Kennedy is assassinated the day before.

The Irish experience their fifth consecutive non-winning season.

1964

9-1-0

Ara Parseghian, who had revitalized the football program at Northwestern after a stellar tenure at Miami (Ohio), takes the Notre Dame coaching job.

Senior quarterback John Huarte, who had played only sparingly in 1962 and 1963, emerges as a first-rate talent and sparks the surprising Fighting Irish to victories in their first nine games and a No. 1 national ranking. In a Cinderella story, he wins the Heisman Trophy.

Huarte and receiver **Jack Snow** are consensus All-Americans.

Huarte throws for 2,062 yards and 16 touchdowns; Snow sets school records for receptions (60), receiving yards (1,114) and touchdown catches (nine).

Huarte and Nick Eddy team up on a 91-yard TD pass against Pittsburgh.

Needing a win over Southern California in their season finale to wrap up the national championship, the Irish lead, 17-0, at halftime but wind up 20-17 losers. USC scores the winning TD on a 15-yard pass from Craig Fertig to Rod Sherman with 1:33 to play.

The Irish finish third in both wire-service polls (by now, United Press is United Press International).

1965

7-2-1

Guard Dick Arrington and safety/return specialist Nick Rassas are consensus All-Americans.

Rassas establishes a Notre Dame season record with 459 punt-return yards and averages 19.1 yards per runback. He also intercepts six passes in '65 and sets a school mark with 197 yards in interception returns.

Halfback Bill Wolski scores five touchdowns against Pittsburgh.

1966

9-0-1

The Fighting Irish are national champs.

Halfback **Eddy**, guard Tom Regner, defensive end Alan Page and linebacker Jim Lynch are consensus All-Americans.

Jim Seymour establishes Notre Dame records for catches (13)

EDDY

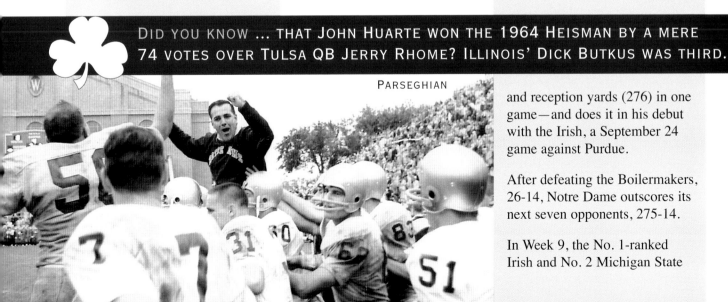

PARSEGHIAN

and reception yards (276) in one game—and does it in his debut with the Irish, a September 24 game against Purdue.

After defeating the Boilermakers, 26-14, Notre Dame outscores its next seven opponents, 275-14.

In Week 9, the No. 1-ranked Irish and No. 2 Michigan State

meet in one of the most talked-about games (before and after) in college football history. The teams fight to a 10-10 tie in a game in which Parseghian is criticized for his conservative late-game play-calling.

A 51-0 destruction of Southern California the next week makes the Irish No. 1 in both season-ending polls. (UPI had dropped Notre Dame to second the week after the Michigan State game.)

1967
8-2-0
Safety Tom Schoen is a consensus All-American.

Quarterback Terry Hanratty throws for a Notre Dame-record 366 yards against Purdue but the Fighting Irish lose, 28-21.

The Irish win their 500th game, beating Georgia Tech by a 36-3 score.

UPI ranks the Irish fourth and AP lists Notre Dame as No. 5.

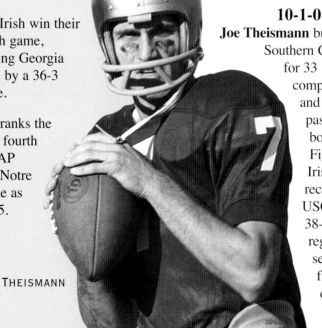

THEISMANN

1968
7-2-1
Hanratty and tackle George Kunz are consensus All-Americans.

Halfback Bob Gladieux scores a school-record 14 touchdowns.

Notre Dame scores 37.6 points per game.

1969
8-2-1
Notre Dame goes 7-0-1 over its final eight regular-season games and plays in its first bowl game in 45 years. No. 1 Texas edges the Irish, 21-17, in the Cotton Bowl.

Joe Theismann throws for 13 touchdowns.

Tom Gatewood hauls in eight TD passes.

Defensive tackle Mike McCoy is a consensus All-American.

The Irish finish fifth in the AP poll and ninth in the UPI balloting.

1970
10-1-0
Joe Theismann burns Southern California for 33 completions and 526 yards passing, both Fighting Irish records. But USC wins, 38-28, in the regular-season finale and dashes

previously unbeaten Notre Dame's hopes for a national title.

Receiver Gatewood and guard Larry DiNardo are consensus All-Americans.

Theismann's 2,429 aerial yards are an all-time Irish best.

In a Cotton Bowl rematch, the Irish upset Texas (again ranked No. 1), 24-11.

Gatewood sets Irish season records with 77 receptions and 1,123 receiving yards.

Notre Dame finishes second, behind Nebraska, in the final AP poll.

1971
8-2-0
Defensive end Walt Patulski and defensive back Clarence Ellis are consensus All-Americans.

Only Southern California and LSU score more than seven points against the Irish—and they deal Notre Dame its only two losses. USC wins, 28-14, in Week 6 and LSU rolls, 28-8, in the season finale.

Gatewood has 33 receptions and ends his career with an Irish record of 157 catches.

1972
8-3-0
Defensive tackle Greg Marx is a consensus All-American.

Cornerback Mike Townsend intercepts 10 passes, a Notre Dame season record.

Southern California's Anthony Davis scores six touchdowns as the No. 1 Trojans blitz Notre Dame, 45-23, in the regular-

season finale. Two of Davis' TDs come on kickoff returns of 96 and 97 yards.

Having played in the Rose Bowl once and the Cotton Bowl twice, Notre Dame makes its first Orange Bowl appearance. Heisman Trophy winner Johnny Rodgers scores four touchdowns and passes for another as Nebraska wallops the Irish, 40-6, in Miami.

1973

11-0-0

The Irish are the AP's national champs after completing a perfect season, one capped by a 24-23 victory over top-ranked Alabama in the Sugar Bowl. **Tom Clements'** clutch passing earns the Irish quarterback Sugar Bowl MVP honors.

The appearance in the New Orleans bowl is a first for Notre Dame.

CLEMENTS

The Irish dominate in the regular season, outscoring opponents by an average of 35.8 points to 6.6. Townsend and tight end Dave Casper are consensus All-Americans.

The unbeaten, untied season is Notre Dame's first since 1949.

1974

10-2-0

Luther Bradley, Ross Browner, Al Hunter and Willie Fry are among Notre Dame players suspended for the '74 season because of disciplinary reasons.

Notre Dame takes a 9-1 record into its regular-season finale at Southern California. The Fighting Irish jump ahead of the Trojans, 24-0, then are devastated by a USC spree of 55 consecutive points. The Trojans' Anthony Davis scores four touchdowns in the game, which ends 55-24.

The Irish rebound in the Orange Bowl, upsetting Alabama, 13-11, and ruining the previously unbeaten Crimson Tide's hopes for the national title. Reggie Barnett's late-game interception seals the victory for Notre Dame, which is playing its last game under the retirement-bound

Parseghian.

Receiver Pete Demmerle and guard Gerry DiNardo are consensus All-Americans.

1975

8-3-0

Dan Devine, who had coached the Green Bay Packers the previous four seasons, is Notre Dame's new coach.

Cornerback Bradley returns an interception 99 yards for a touchdown against Purdue in Week 2. The Fighting Irish win, 17-0.

Tony Dorsett breaks loose for 303 rushing yards as Pittsburgh defeats Notre Dame, 34-20.

Defensive tackle Steve Niehaus is a consensus All-American.

Daniel "Rudy" Ruettiger, 27, a student who had long dreamed of playing for Notre Dame and talked himself onto the scout team at Irish practices, sees brief action against Georgia Tech in the final home game of the season.

1976

9-3-0

Defensive end Browner wins the Outland Trophy.

Browner and tight end **Ken MacAfee** are consensus All-Americans.

Dave Reeve kicks a school-record 53-yard field goal against Pittsburgh, but the Panthers are 31-10 winners.

Hunter becomes Notre Dame's first 1,000-yard rusher. He finishes with 1,058 yards.

Hunter's 102 yards on the ground and two touchdowns help the Irish past Penn State, 20-9, in the Gator Bowl.

1977

11-1-0

The Fighting Irish win the national championship.

After losing to Mississippi in Week 2, Notre Dame wins 10 straight games. No. 10 is a 38-10 upset of top-ranked Texas in the Cotton Bowl, a victory that vaults the No. 5 Irish to the top.

On October 22, the Irish come out in green jerseys against Southern California. With players and fans alike fired up at Notre Dame Stadium, Devine's team crushes USC, 49-19. Notre Dame wears the jerseys the rest of the season.

MacAfee (54 receptions), Browner and Bradley are consensus All-Americans.

Fullback Jerome Heavens runs for 994 yards.

Bradley intercepts five passes, giving him a Fighting Irish career record of 17.

1978

9-3-0

Vagas Ferguson rushes for a school-record 255 yards against Georgia Tech. He carries the ball 30 times.

Ferguson becomes Notre Dame's second 1,000-yard rusher, gaining 1,192 yards.

Linebacker Bob Golic and center Dave Huffman are consensus All-Americans.

Trailing Houston, 34-12, in the fourth quarter of the Cotton Bowl, the Joe Montana-led Irish shock the Cougars with three touchdowns, a pair of two-point conversions and a point-after kick in the final $7\frac{1}{2}$ minutes and win, 35-34.

Montana finishes with 4,121 yards passing and 25 TD passes over his three varsity seasons.

1979

7-4-0

Ferguson sets a Notre Dame single-season rushing record with 1,437 yards and is the first Fighting Irish player to record two 1,000-yard seasons.

Ferguson is a consensus All-American.

The four losses are the most in a season for Notre Dame since the 1963 team suffered seven defeats.

Linebacker Bob Crable sets a school record with 187 tackles.

The Irish play their season finale in Tokyo, where they drub

MONTANA

Miami (Fla.), 40-15. Dave Waymer returns two interceptions for touchdowns against the Hurricanes.

1980

9-2-1

Harry Oliver's 51-yard field goal as time expires lifts the Irish past Michigan, 29-27.

Phil Carter threatens Ferguson's single-game Irish rushing record with a 254-yard performance against Michigan State.

Only a tie with Georgia Tech sullies Notre Dame's record entering the regular-season finale at Southern California. But the No. 2 Irish lose to the Trojans, 20-3.

Herschel Walker runs for two

FERGUSON

DID YOU KNOW ... THAT VAGAS FERGUSON CARRIED THE BALL A NOTRE DAME-RECORD 301 TIMES IN 1979?

touchdowns and 150 yards as No. 1 Georgia defeats the Irish, 17-10, in the Sugar Bowl. It is Devine's last game as Notre Dame coach.

Notre Dame finishes ninth (AP) and 10th (UPI) in the polls.

Crable and center John Scully are consensus All-Americans.

1981

5-6-0

Gerry Faust jumps from the Ohio high school coaching ranks to the top job at Notre Dame. Faust had fashioned a 174-17-2 record in 18 seasons at Moeller High in Cincinnati.

Faust breaks in with a victory, 27-9 over Louisiana State, but his Irish drop four of their next five games.

Greg Bell goes 98 yards for a kickoff-return TD against Miami (Fla.).

Quarterback Blair Kiel and split end Joe Howard connect on an Irish-record 96-yard pass play against Georgia Tech.

Crable is a consensus All-American.

1982

6-4-1

In the first night game ever played at Notre Dame Stadium, the Irish edge Michigan, 23-17,

in the season opener. Dave Duerson's late-game interception sews up the victory.

After starting the season 4-0, the Fighting Irish go 2-4-1 the rest of the way.

Duerson picks off three passes against Navy.

For the first time since 1963, Notre Dame does not have a consensus All-American.

1983

7-5-0

Tailback Allen Pinkett rushes for 1,394 yards.

A five-game midseason winning streak and a 19-18 triumph over Doug Flutie and Boston College in the Liberty Bowl stand out.

1984

7-5-0

Defeats continue to come with startling frequency. The Fighting Irish lose three straight in one stretch.

Pinkett gains 1,105 yards on the ground.

Mark Bavaro makes a team-high 32 receptions.

SMU edges Notre Dame, 27-20, in the Aloha Bowl.

1985

5-6-0

Faust resigns as coach with one game remaining. His resignation is effective after the season finale at Miami (Fla.).

The Faust era ends with a

PINKETT

crushing 58-7 loss to the Hurricanes.

Pinkett gains 1,100 yards and becomes the first Irish player to rush for more than 1,000 yards in three consecutive seasons.

Pinkett ends his Irish career with a Notre Dame-record 53 touchdowns.

1986

5-6-0

Lou Holtz, who had coached at Minnesota in 1984 and 1985 after a highly successful tenure at Arkansas, replaces Faust.

 DID YOU KNOW ... THAT, BEGINNING IN 1983, THE IRISH DEFEATED USC 11 CONSECUTIVE TIMES AND WERE 12-0-1 VS. THE TROJANS FROM 1983-95?

HOLTZ

The Irish have back-to-back losing seasons for the first time since their first two years (1887, 1888) of fielding a football team.

Holtz's first season ends on a high note as Notre Dame, down 37-20 early in the fourth quarter, rallies for a 38-37 win at Southern California. John Carney's 19-yard field goal at the gun wins it. **Steve Beuerlein** throws for four touchdowns against USC.

1987
8-4-0

Brown wins the Heisman Trophy and is a consensus All-American.

Against Michigan State in Week 2, **Brown** scores on 71- and 66-yard punt returns in a span of

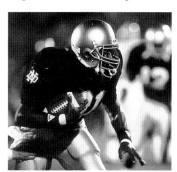

two minutes. He accumulates 275 all-purpose yards as Notre Dame routs the Spartans, 31-8.

Brown is a season-long quadruple threat as a receiver, rusher, punt returner and kickoff-return man.

The Irish are 8-1 after walloping Alabama, 37-6, but they lose their final

Raghib "Rocket" Ismail returns two kickoffs for touchdowns against Rice, traveling 87 and 83 yards.

Notre Dame, which takes over the No. 1 spot in early November, nails down the top ranking by whipping West Virginia, 34-21, in the Fiesta Bowl.

Defensive end Frank Stams and linebacker Michael Stonebreaker are consensus All-Americans.

1989
12-1-0

For the second time in his career, **Ismail** returns two kickoffs for touchdowns in one game. This time, he victimizes Michigan on 88- and 92-yard scoring jaunts as Notre Dame wins, 24-19, in Ann Arbor.

DID YOU KNOW ... THAT THE IRISH HAVE PLAYED VIRGINIA ONLY ONCE, BEATING THE CAVALIERS IN 1989?

Beuerlein passes for 2,211 yards and 13 touchdowns in '86.

Flanker Tim Brown catches 45 passes for 910 yards and five TDs and averages 27.9 yards on kickoff returns.

Brown scores on kickoff returns of 96 yards (against LSU) and 95 yards (Air Force).

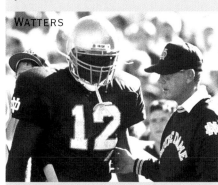

WATTERS

three games to Penn State, Miami (Fla.) and Texas A&M (Cotton Bowl).

1988
12-0-0

The Irish are national champs.

Reggie Ho's 26-yard field goal with 1:13 to play beats Michigan, 19-17, in the nighttime season opener in South Bend. **Ricky Watters** scores on an 81-yard punt return against the Wolverines.

Notre Dame jolts No. 1 Miami (Fla.), 31-30, in Week 6 and rolls through the regular season undefeated.

ISMAIL

Watters' 97-yard punt return against SMU is the longest in Fighting Irish history.

The Irish win their first 11 games and take a school-record 23-game winning streak into the regular-season finale at Miami

(Fla.). The Hurricanes upset the top-ranked Irish, 27-10.

Notre Dame pulls an upset of its own in the Orange Bowl, stopping No. 1 Colorado, 21-6.

Cornerback **Todd Lyght** and defensive tackle Chris Zorich are consensus All-Americans.

AP ranks the Irish No. 2; UPI voters list them third.

1990
9-3-0

Notre Dame takes an 8-1 record and a No. 1 ranking into Week 10 but falls to Penn State, 24-21. Craig Fayak's 34-yard field goal in the closing seconds topples the Irish.

Colorado wins half of the national championship—the AP version—by edging Notre Dame, 10-9, in the Orange Bowl. Ismail's 91-yard punt return near game's end is called back because of a penalty, enabling the Buffaloes to escape defeat.

Georgia Tech wins the UPI national title.

Lyght, Stonebreaker, **Zorich** and wide receiver/ return specialist Ismail win consensus All-American honors.

Craig Hentrich kicks a school-record five field goals against Miami (Fla.).

Notre Dame finishes sixth in both polls.

This is the last season that UPI conducts the official coaches poll. Starting in 1991, USA Today/CNN gets the honor (and in 1997, USA Today/ESPN takes over).

1991
10-3-0

NBC begins exclusive television coverage of Notre Dame home games. In the first game of the five-year, $38 million package, the Fighting Irish dump Indiana, 49-27, as quarterback **Rick Mirer** runs for three touchdowns and throws for another.

BETTIS

DID YOU KNOW ... THAT NOTRE DAME POSTED ITS 700TH VICTORY WITH A TRIUMPH OVER NAVY IN 1991?

MIRER

Mirer sets a Notre Dame season record with 18 TD passes.

Many critics consider the 18th-ranked Irish undeserving of a bid to a major bowl. Unfazed, the Irish take on No. 3 Florida in the Sugar Bowl and whip the Gators, 39-28. **Jerome Bettis** scores three fourth-quarter touchdowns as Notre Dame strikes for 32 second-half points.

Guard Mirko Jurkovic wins consensus All-American honors.

Bettis scores a Notre Dame-record 20 touchdowns.

1992
10-1-1

The Fighting Irish win their last seven games, capping the run with a 28-3 triumph over Texas A&M in the Cotton Bowl.

Reggie Brooks rushes for 1,343 yards and Bettis rumbles for 825.

Brooks gains 7.6 yards per carry in his Notre Dame career (198 attempts, 1,508 yards).

BROOKS

Mirer throws for 15 TDs in '92.

Guard Aaron Taylor wins consensus All-American honors.

1993

11-1-0

The last two weeks of the regular season offer high drama. First, the No. 2 Fighting Irish upend No. 1 Florida State, 31-24, and seize the top ranking for themselves. Then the Irish give up the top spot in an agonizing 41-39 loss to Boston College.

Notre Dame defeats Texas A&M, 24-21, in the Cotton Bowl.

The Irish finish No. 2 in both polls.

Taylor and safety Jeff Burris win consensus All-American honors.

Lee Becton rushes for 1,044 yards.

Clint Johnson burns Stanford on a 100-yard kickoff return.

The motion picture "Rudy," the inspirational story of 1975 Notre Dame player Rudy Ruettiger, opens in theaters nationwide.

1994

6-5-1

Freshman quarterback **Ron Powlus** throws 19 touchdown passes, a Fighting Irish record.

Derrick Mayes' 11 TD receptions are the most in one season in school history.

Cornerback Bobby Taylor wins consensus All-American honors.

Notre Dame starts the season 4-1 but stumbles to a 2-4-1 finish that includes a 41-24 loss to Colorado in the Fiesta Bowl.

1995

9-3-0

Notre Dame wins its final six regular-season games.

With Powlus sidelined because of a broken arm and leading rusher Randy Kinder out because of disciplinary reasons, the Fighting Irish face a tough

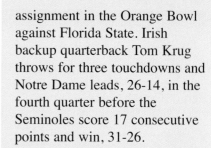

assignment in the Orange Bowl against Florida State. Irish backup quarterback Tom Krug throws for three touchdowns and Notre Dame leads, 26-14, in the fourth quarter before the Seminoles score 17 consecutive points and win, 31-26.

Mayes finishes his career as the school's all-time leader in reception yards (2,512) and TD catches (22).

1996

8-3-0

Holtz begins his 11th season as Notre Dame coach, tying for the second-longest tenure behind Rockne's 13 years on the job. Leahy and Parseghian also served 11 years.

Allen Rossum scores on a 99-yard kickoff return against Purdue.

Overtime is introduced in college football in 1996, and the Fighting Irish play their first overtime game on October 19 against Air Force. The Falcons win, 20-17.

Notre Dame and Navy play in Dublin, Ireland. The Irish breeze, 54-27.

DID YOU KNOW ... THAT THE 1996 SEASON OPENER AGAINST VANDERBILT WAS THE 1,000TH GAME IN IRISH HISTORY?

DENSON

1997

7-6-0

Davie is a winner his first time out—the Fighting Irish edge Georgia Tech, 17-13—but he and the Irish lose their next four games.

The Georgia Tech game is the first one in expanded Notre Dame Stadium, where seating capacity goes from 59,075 to 80,225 (and eventually reaches 80,795).

For the first time in school history, Notre Dame plays without a penalty or a turnover. The error-free performance comes in a 24-6 victory at Louisiana State.

Powlus completes 14 consecutive passes against Michigan State, a Notre Dame record, but most are short-yardage throws as the Irish lose, 23-7.

Powlus connects for nine touchdowns through the air and

DID YOU KNOW ... THAT AMONG THE COACHES WHO SPENT AT LEAST FIVE SEASONS AT NOTRE DAME, GERRY FAUST (.535) AND BOB DAVIE (.583) HAVE THE LOWEST WINNING PERCENTAGES?

Holtz announces on November 19 that this is his last season as Irish coach. Four days later, he wins for the 100th and last time at Notre Dame in a 62-0 pounding of Rutgers.

Powlus throws for four touchdowns in the Rutgers game. It is the third four-TD passing game of his career.

In Holtz's final game, the Irish lose in overtime to Southern California, 27-20, in Los Angeles.

Autry Denson runs for 1,179 yards.

Defensive coordinator **Bob Davie** is named Holtz's successor.

EXPANDED NOTRE DAME STADIUM

completes his career with a school-mark 52 TD passes. His career passing-yardage figure of 7,602 also is a Notre Dame record.

A five-game winning streak earns the Irish a berth in the Independence Bowl, where they lose a rematch with LSU, 27-9.

1998

9-3-0

Denson tops 1,000 yards rushing for the third consecutive season, finishing his career with a Notre Dame-record 4,318 yards on the ground.

Notre Dame wins eight consecutive games but loses at Southern California, 10-0, in the regular-season finale.

The Irish break out green jerseys for their Gator Bowl game against Georgia Tech, but Notre Dame comes up short, 35-28.

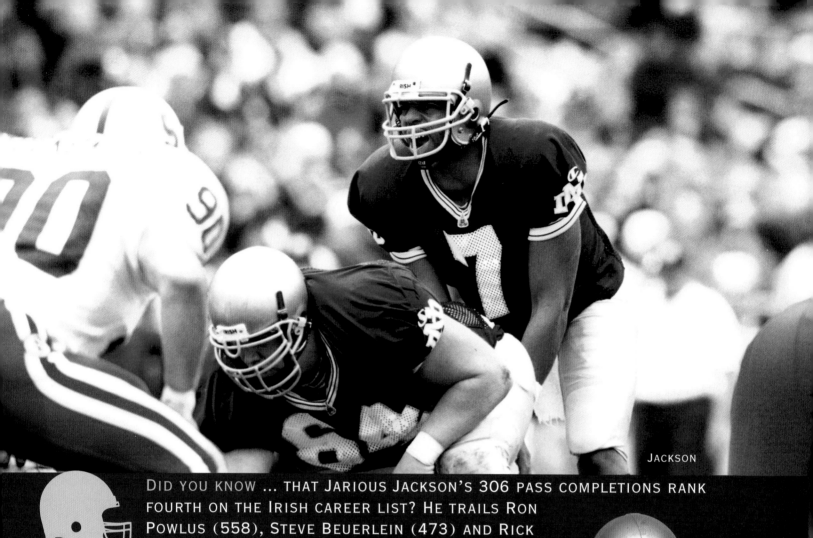

JACKSON

1999

5-7-0

Quarterback **Jarious Jackson** establishes Notre Dame season passing records for completions (184), attempts (316) and yards (2,753).

Jackson burns the Arizona State defense for four TD passes.

There is scoring aplenty in '99, with the Fighting Irish averaging 29 points and their opponents 27.6.

2000

9-3-0

For the second straight year, Notre Dame and its opponents score in double figures in every regular-season game.

Eric Crouch's seven-yard TD run in overtime lifts No. 1 Nebraska past the Fighting Irish, 27-24, at Notre Dame Stadium. The stadium is a sea of red, much to the consternation of Irish coaches and players. Nebraska fans, known as great travelers, buy thousands of tickets from Notre Dame partisans willing to give them up.

Julius Jones scores on a 100-yard kickoff return against the Cornhuskers.

The Fighting Irish take a seven-game winning streak into their Fiesta Bowl match against Oregon State. In the teams' first-ever meeting, the Beavers erupt for 29 third-quarter points and rip the Irish, 41-9.

2001

5-6-0

Notre Dame manages only two touchdowns in its first three games and begins the season 0-3.

Davie is dismissed on December 2, one day after the Fighting Irish conclude the season with a 24-18 victory over Purdue.

The Irish and Boilermakers usually square off early in the season, but the September 11 terrorist attacks in the United States force a postponement of their scheduled September 15 game.

Vontez Duff races 96 yards for a kickoff-return TD against Purdue.

George O'Leary, coach at Georgia Tech since 1995, is introduced as Davie's successor on December 9 but resigns five days later after admitting that his resume contained errors about his academic and athletic background.

2002

10-3-0

Tyrone Willingham is introduced as Notre Dame's new coach on January 1. He had been Stanford's coach for seven seasons.

The Fighting Irish don't score an offensive touchdown until the third game of the season, but they ride a stingy and opportunistic defense to an 8-0 record.

Boston College defeats the Irish, 14-7, to snap the winning streak, and Southern California shreds Notre Dame, 44-13, in the regular-season finale. USC's Carson Palmer passes for 425 yards, a record for a Notre Dame opponent.

In the Gator Bowl, the Irish are beaten by North Carolina State, 28-6. It is the sixth consecutive bowl loss for Notre Dame.

Cornerback **Shane Walton** is Notre Dame's first consensus All-American in eight years.

Walton intercepts three passes in the Kickoff Classic opener against Maryland and Nick Setta equals an Irish record with five field goals against the Terrapins.

Notre Dame beats Navy for the 39th consecutive time.

GRANT

Ryan Grant rushes for 1,085 yards.

The Fighting Irish end their 114th season with an all-time record of 791-250-42 over 1,083 games. Their winning percentage of .750 ranks No. 1 in NCAA Division I-A.

DUFF

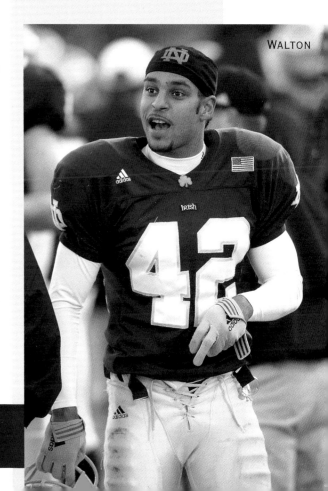

WALTON

DID YOU KNOW ... THAT NOTRE DAME IS 123-22-5 AGAINST ARMY, AIR FORCE AND NAVY?